The Whole Christ for the Whole World

The Whole Christ for the Whole World
A Wesleyan Perspective on the Work of Christ

H. Ray Dunning

WIPF & STOCK · Eugene, Oregon

THE WHOLE CHRIST FOR THE WHOLE WORLD
A Wesleyan Perspective on the Work of Christ

Copyright © 2008 H. Ray Dunning. All rights reserved. Except for brief quotations in critical publications or reviews, no part of this book may be reproduced in any manner without prior written permission from the publisher. Write: Permissions, Wipf and Stock, 199 W. 8th Ave., Suite 3, Eugene, OR 97401.

ISBN 13: 978-1-55635-267-6

Manufactured in the U.S.A.

Contents

1. Introduction / 1
2. Formation of the Eastern Perspective / 13
3. Development of the Western Tradition / 23
4. The Atonement in Protestant Theology / 39
5. Responses to "Orthodoxy" / 49
6. Atonement: Objective or Subjective / 63
7. Changing Emphases in Atonement Theology / 75
8. Insights from Biblical Theology / 89
9. The Rhythm of Redemption / 107
10. The Holy Spirit and the Atonement / 121

Bibliography / 131

1

Introduction

"Paradigm" and "paradigm shift" are familiar terms today, thanks in part to the work of Thomas Kuhn in the field of natural science. These tools have been useful as a way of interpreting the history of theology, which may be seen as a series of paradigm shifts.[1] This approach is certainly *apropos* to theological methodology, the understanding of the divine nature and many other issues central to the theological task. It is critically important for understanding the history of theological reflection about the work of Christ. Perhaps in no other area has the influence of culture been more pronounced than in the shifting paradigms of atonement theories. Numerous scholars have called attention to this factor in shaping various explanations of the work of Christ. But as R. Larry Shelton says:

> While these theories have been useful within their cultural contexts, the very fact that they have arisen out of specific cultural/historical settings has tended to limit the universality of their relevance. Theological creativity in expressing the Gospel in relevant cultural terms is to be encouraged, but the freezing of some of these theories into creedal and dogmatic forms tends to diminish their effectiveness when the cultural and historical milieu changes.[2]

This interplay between theology and culture has both strengths and weaknesses, as Shelton's comment suggests. One major strength lies in the possibility of contextualizing the Christian message, a possibility that is justified by the fact that unlike certain other central Christian beliefs, there was no orthodox doctrine approved by the undivided church. One weakness lies in the danger that thought-forms derived from culture may distort the truth in diverse ways.

An important source for the variety of so-called atonement theories is the fact that there is such a diversity of images in the New Testament itself. This variety of metaphors may be explained in terms of the perception of

1. King, "The Task of Theology," 1–27.
2. Shelton, "A Covenant Concept of Atonement," 100.

the human predicament by those to whom the messages were addressed (as well as by the writer). In order to get some sense of the wide variety of concepts in the scripture, we may note a very generalized taxonomy of the way the major segments of the New Testament view the work of Christ.

In the Synoptic Gospels, Jesus is seen as the one who brings in the Kingdom of God (or heaven [Matthew]) by overpowering the demonic powers that control this age through living out the vision of the servant ideal pictured in Isaiah 40–55. In this imagery, sin is seen as bondage.

In the Fourth Gospel, Jesus is described as the one who brings light, life and truth by revealing the Father. Sin is to be in darkness and death.

With Paul, Jesus is the one who reconciles humanity to God, offering acceptance through the righteousness of God and through his Spirit renewing his people in the divine image. Sin is alienation from God and one's created destiny.

In the letter to the Hebrews, the Son is the one who "tastes death for every man." This metaphor is alluded to only briefly but here sin is standing under the penalty of death. More centrally, Jesus is interpreted as the perfect priest and sacrifice whose work perfects his people (sanctification). Sin in this context is cultic impurity. As Donald Baillie correctly notes, "The initial function of sin-offerings and guilt-offerings in Israel was the wiping out of ceremonial offences."[3] Since it is the cultic rituals of Israel that inform the theology of Hebrews related to sin, this has important implications for a full canonical interpretation of the work of Christ.

The book of Revelation depicts Jesus as the one who restores all things to their divinely appointed destiny by bringing to consummation the victory he won through his suffering during his earthly ministry. In this sense, while its literary form may be apocalyptic, its theology is not.

An important principle of interpretation that should be mentioned here is that metaphors in the New Testament used to describe the results of the work of Christ are drawn chiefly from the Old Testament: reconciliation, justification, sanctification, salvation, redemption, etc. As Ronald Wallace says: "We cannot fully understand what they [the writers] were saying unless we try to interpret precisely what these words meant within the contexts in which they were used."[4] And the conceptual context is primarily the Old Testament, not Greek philosophy, Roman law, or pagan usage.

Anyone who believes that his or her proposal is the final word is simply failing to recognize the human character of theological constructs. However, one important stipulation must be honored, at least from my

---

3. Baillie, *God Was in Christ*, 175.
4. Wallace, *The Atoning Death of Christ*, 32.

Introduction

point of view. The adequacy of any explanation of the work of Christ should be constantly tested by scripture seen in its wholeness rather than by proof-texting dogmatic conclusions.

A number of other factors have been influential in theologizing about the work of Christ. Perhaps the most important for the Western church (both Roman Catholic and Protestant) has been an intellectual perspective formed by juridical modes of thought. Many scholars have taken notice of this fact.[5] This perspective has resulted in interpretations that tend to limit the doctrine of the atonement in at least two major ways:

1) with regard to its inclusiveness and
2) with regard to the extent of its redemptive provision.

While these limitations will occupy our primary attention in the subsequent analyses, there are also other factors that have called into question the dominant evangelical doctrine of the work of Christ in the West. The challenge of post-modernism has raised numerous issues.[6] A charge from the feminist perspective that the penal satisfaction theory of the atonement implicitly approves child abuse and other forms of patriarchal violence is widely discussed.[7] From within the evangelical tradition itself, various theological charges have been leveled. It has been questioned on the grounds that it entails a mistaken doctrine of God,[8] that it conflicts with the orthodox doctrine of the trinity by setting the persons of the trinity against each other,[9] and that it thrives in the soil of modern Western individualism.[10] Each issue no doubt deserves extensive consideration. However my purpose is to examine the evangelical tradition from the perspective of Wesleyan theology, which brings some of them only peripherally into view.

Beyond mere analysis, I propose to explore the possibilities of a paradigm that I call the *personal-relational paradigm*. It is my belief that this model best reflects the "whole tenor of scripture" (John Wesley's term) in the light of the present findings of biblical theology. I am further con-

---

5. Dabney, "Justified by the Spirit"; Gonzalez, *Christian Thought Revisited*.

6. Mann, *Atonement for a "Sinless Society."*

7. Brown and Bohn, *Christianity, Patriarchy, and Abuse*; Parker and Brock, *Proverbs of Ashes*; Swartley, *Violence Renounced*; Weaver, *The Non-violent Atonement*.

8. Travis, *Christ and the Judgment of God*; Green and Baker, *Recovering the Scandal of the Cross*.

9. Sykes, "Outline of a Theology of Sacrifice."

10. Green and Baker, *Recovering the Scandal of the Cross*.

vinced that this paradigm is the most appropriate one to inform preaching in the contemporary situation.

The limitation relating to the redemptive provisions of the dominant evangelical way of interpreting the work of Christ referred to above became obvious to me out of the attempt to develop a systematic theology from a Wesleyan perspective. A number of factors came to light that intensified my realization that as a Wesleyan I could not consistently accept certain traditional evangelical options about the work of Christ because of their restrictive implications. More importantly, I found these to be, at best, in tension with biblical theology as I had come to understand it, if not in outright contradiction.

The Wesleyan Norm

In some ways the most decisive element in the task of developing a systematic theology was the attempt to identify the norm of the Wesleyan perspective. While there had been a long history of theological writings in this tradition, since John Fletcher's initial attempt[11] these had basically been compendia, primarily dealing with all or most of the Christian doctrines but without identifying a unifying perspective (norm).

After many years of teaching courses in systematic theology using a variety of approaches, I eventually came to the conviction that the heart of the Wesleyan perspective is soteriology, visualized as an ellipse with two foci rather than as a single doctrine or theme.[12] These foci were justification and sanctification seen in a polar tension with each other. While there were other elements involved that gave a particular character to this ellipse, the polar relation between these two soteriological doctrines gave Wesleyan theology its unique place in the history of Christian thought.

That John Wesley himself thought about the uniqueness of his message in this way is seen in a quotation from his sermon "On God's Vineyard":

> It is, then, a great blessing given to this people, that as they do not think or speak of justification so as to supersede sanctification, so neither do they speak of sanctification so as to supersede justification. They take care to keep each in its own place, laying equal stress on one and the other. They know God has joined these

---

11. Fletcher developed Wesleyan theology by way of the formative concept of prevenient grace, which was central to that perspective. See John A. Knight, "The Theology of John Fletcher."

12. Dunning, "Perspective for a Wesleyan Systematic Theology."

together, and it is not for man to put them asunder. Therefore they maintain, with equal zeal and diligence, the doctrine of free, full, present justification on the one hand, and of entire sanctification both of heart and life on the other, being as tenacious of inward holiness as any Mystic, and of outward, as any Pharisee.[13]

One of the leading Wesley scholars in the twentieth century, Albert Outler, had affirmed this same interpretation in only a slightly different way. He saw the genius of Wesley to be the persistent holding together of "faith alone" and "holy living" and resisting all polarizations toward one or the other. He says: "It is in terms of his success and failure in *this* attempt . . . that we may speak of Wesley's place in the Christian tradition . . . This particular linkage between *sola fide* (justification) and 'holy living' (sanctification) has no precedent, to my knowledge, anywhere in classical Protestantism."[14]

The point at issue is that, from the Wesleyan perspective, any interpretation of the work of Christ that fails to make provision for both justification and sanctification would be inadequate. It is clear that both are benefits identified in the New Testament as the heritage of the believer in Jesus Christ. On this basis we have a criterion by which to evaluate proposed explanations of the soteriological provisions of the atonement.

John Wesley's Teaching on the Atonement

A somewhat disturbing factor in this pursuit was the awareness that Wesley himself appeared to hold to some form of the satisfaction view of the atonement, while at the same time fighting against its implications based on his central soteriological commitments.[15] Randy Maddox takes note of the same tension. Due to the eclectic nature of his Anglican context, says Maddox, Wesley was exposed to three varieties of the view but he appears to be most in conversation with the substitutionary justification view of Luther and Calvin, while constantly rejecting its logical implications.[16] I had come to see that to be Wesleyan in the contemporary situation was not to slavishly follow everything that John Wesley taught (or appeared to teach), but to be faithful to the presuppositional insights about soteriological matters that constituted the genius of this tradition.[17]

13. Wesley, *The Works of John Wesley*, 7:205.
14. Outler, "The Place of Wesley in the Christian Tradition," 39.
15. Renshaw, "The Atonement in the Theology of John and Charles Wesley."
16. Cf. Maddox, *Responsible Grace*, 102–6.
17. Deshner suggested that we would do well to judge Wesley, as far as possible, accord-

It has been generally recognized that one of the reasons for Wesley's use of satisfaction language was the fact that he was no systematic theologian and furthermore wrote no sermon or treatise on the atonement. It has been suggested that his sermon on "The Lord our Righteousness" qualifies as an atonement sermon. But while this sermon has implications for the atonement, it is essentially a refutation of Wesley's critics who had accused him of being a Papist, that is, one who bases salvation on works-righteousness. This accusation arose out of Wesley's emphasis on holiness of life as essential to Christian experience. In defense, he insisted that he taught justification based on the imputed righteousness of Christ, but he argued that this did not lead to antinomianism as he felt was the case with his opponents who made much of the active and passive righteousness of Christ. In later years, Wesley expressed regret in using the term "imputed righteousness" because it was widely misunderstood to mean "imputed obedience" thus resulting in antinomianism.[18] Hence he refused to distinguish between the passive and active righteousness of Christ, insisting that it was the former that was the basis of justification.[19] But this concession is instructive in recognizing how profoundly he was influenced by the view that salvation is based on ethical righteousness, even if imputed as an alien righteousness, a view that has plagued the Western church from the second century. We shall explore this in some depth throughout the study.

Throughout his writings, there appears three major issues that bothered Wesley about the implications of the prevailing satisfaction interpretations of the work of Christ, and consequently of the view itself even if he did not express his concerns as such:

    1) The nature of God. Most versions of the satisfaction interpretation are based on the idea that the essential nature of God is sovereign will, or justice. Wesley, to the contrary, asserts that nowhere in scripture is it said that "God is Justice," but it does say "God is Love."[20]

    2) The universality of the atonement or the question of the inclusiveness of grace. The inescapable logical implication of the satisfaction view is either universalism or limited atonement. Naturally, the latter position was adopted

---

ing to his *intention*, *Wesley's Christology*, 196.

  18. Wesley, *Works*, 10:430.

  19. Deschner, *Wesley's Christology*, 152–57.

  20. Wesley, *Works*, 10:227; *Notes on the New Testament* on 1 John 4:8.

Introduction

and Wesley found this to be in gross contradiction to the teachings of scripture.[21]

3) The centrality of the holy life. Here was Wesley's most vigorous point of opposition because of his profound commitment to holy living (sanctification). If one takes the satisfaction view with full seriousness, it logically leads to the conclusion that the holy life is inconsequential. While at least some of its advocates struggled to find a place for the necessity of holiness, the real bite was taken from the effort.

Although somewhat repetitive, my opinions were reinforced by the fact that other theologians in the Wesleyan tradition had called attention to the incompatibility between the satisfaction theory and the central soteriological commitments of Wesleyan theology. One of the most insightful observations on this matter was made by J. Glenn Gould in his small work, *The Precious Blood of Christ*. He says: "Perhaps there is a basic inconsistency between Wesley's hazily defined doctrine of the atonement and his clearly stated doctrine of prevenient grace."[22] Unfortunately he did not develop the implications of this inconsistency.

Virtually all other Wesleyan theologians had manifested the same reluctance to accept the traditional form of a substitutionary explanation. In an attempt to avoid its implications, most advocated the Governmental theory of Hugo Grotius, a follower of James Arminius. But this view does not escape the presuppositions that informed the Calvinistic theory. Hence there has been considerable ambiguity in their discussions of the atonement.

Albert Outler points out that oddly enough the same ambiguity found in these self-professed Wesleyan theologians is present in the Articles of Faith of the United Methodist Church. As he explained, Wesley did not change the forensic model found in the Anglican Articles and thus it became incorporated in the Methodist Articles thus reversing the Pauline teaching about reconciliation. "Happily," rejoices Outler, "in Article VIII of the former Evangelical United Brethren 'Confession,' we find the original Pauline form, 'God was in Christ reconciling the world to him-

---

21. While it has been argued that John Calvin did not teach a limited atonement, he limited the provisions of the atonement by saying that awakening grace is extended to only the elect with the same unsatisfactory result. This will be explored more fully later on.

22. Gould, *The Precious Blood of Christ*, 75.

self'—which means that somewhat absent-mindedly, United Methodists have it *both* ways!"[23]

How does one account for these inconsistencies in professed Wesleyan theologians? The answer seems rather simple in Outler's example. In general I would suggest that the primary reason was the unexamined assumption regarding the divine-human relation that has been present throughout Western theological history, the same assumption that informed Wesley's inconsistencies about the work of Christ. *The thesis that informs this essay is that when this assumption is identified and evaluated in the light of biblical theology, a dramatically different understanding of this central teaching of the Christian faith will emerge.*

Relation between the "Fact" and the "Manner"

This tension in Wesley and many of his successors raises the question of the relation between the fact and the manner. George Croft Cell in his pioneering study of Wesley's theology said that the atonement, for Wesley, is the "burning focus of faith, . . . comprehensive of the whole meaning of the Gospel, the whole of Christianity."[24] Wesley himself in a letter to a correspondent said, "Indeed, nothing in the Christian system is of greater consequence than the doctrine of the Atonement. It is properly the distinguishing point between Deism and Christianity."[25] In a word, it is certain that the fact of the atonement was crucial for Wesley.

In the light of this, it appears somewhat odd that he wrote the following words in a letter to Mary Bishop, February 7, 1778: "Our reason is here quickly bewildered. If we attempt to expatiate [to speak or write at length] in this field, we 'find no end, in wandering mazes lost.' But the question is (the only question with me; I regard nothing else), What saith the Scripture?"[26]

But as Randy Maddox rightly observed:

> It is one thing to value the Atonement; it is another to explain it. For all of his emphasis on the Atonement, Wesley never provided a prolonged or systematic summary of his understanding of it. His characteristic emphases and concerns must be observed in the vari-

---

23. Outler, *Theology in the Wesleyan Spirit*, 53. The present United Methodist Church is the result of a union of the Methodist Church with the Evangelical United Brethren Church.

24. Cell, *The Rediscovery of John Wesley*, 297.

25. Wesley, *Letters*, 6:197–98.

26. Quoted in Shelton, "Covenant Concept of Atonement," 102.

ous practical-theological contexts where he found consideration of the Atonement necessary.²⁷

While one may distinguish between the fact and the manner, the truth is that it is practically impossible to hold to the fact without some sense of the *modus operandi*. This suggests a principle by which one can evaluate the adequacy of a proposed theory. There must be a systematic relation between christology and soteriology.

Even though Wesley's most explicit language reflected the presuppositions of the satisfaction theory (phrases such as the "meritorious work of Christ," etc.), there were other elements in his thought that could be developed consistently with his basic commitments about human need and the divine provision. These insights are chiefly given expression in his *Notes on the New Testament* and revolve around the three-fold office of Christ as prophet, priest, and king.²⁸ This structure was first centrally used by John Calvin to describe the mediatorial work of Christ and it became standard for subsequent Reformed theologians as well as many others. Wesley's development, minimal though it was, manifested significant similarities to Calvin. However, consistent with his central soteriological commitments he explicitly identified these offices as providing for both justification and sanctification.

Wesley and Eastern Theology

Another factor helping to shape my thinking was the emerging awareness among students of Wesley of the influence of both Eastern and Western modes of thought upon him. The former emphasized the incarnation as the therapeutic aspect of the work of Christ and the latter the death of Christ as providing a forensic justification.²⁹

Concerning Albert Outler's identification of the genius of Wesley to be the persistent holding together of faith alone and holy living referred to above, he further declares that these two emphasize a *via media* between Western (Latin) Christendom and Eastern (Greek) Christendom, the first emphasizing "forensic images, metaphors from the law courts (Roman and medieval)"; the second has been "fascinated by visions of ontological 'participation in God.'"

27. Maddox, *Responsible Grace*, 97.

28. I was initially made aware of this by John Deschner in his *Wesley's Christology* and attempted to develop this structure in *Grace, Faith, and Holiness*.

29. Maddox, "John Wesley and Eastern Orthodoxy." Cf. also Rust, "The Atoning Act of God in Christ."

It is well known that, as a good Anglican, Wesley was deeply influenced by the Greek fathers of the Patristic period and from this well drew many of his distinctive insights about sanctification. Randy Maddox says in the introduction to his definitive work on Wesley's theology:

> My ongoing dialog with Wesley convinced me that he is indeed best understood as one fundamentally committed to the therapeutic view of the Christian life. Demonstrating this primacy, and reflecting on how Wesley integrated the juridical convictions of Western Christianity into his more basic therapeutic viewpoint, has become another major goal of this book.[30]

There is a remarkable parallel between Wesleyan theology and Eastern Orthodoxy at numerous points. Of greatest significance is the way in which the incarnation and the atonement were related in attempting to provide a theological explanation of the work of Christ. In a word, this reinforced my growing conviction that the whole Christ must be involved in atonement theology. Actually the move away from the fragmentation of the gospel that does not incorporate the whole Christ event in theological understanding has been going on in certain quarters with certain scholars for some time and with telling arguments.[31]

As H. Ganse Little has said:

> Once the startling continuity is realized between "God was in Christ" and "Christ died for us" the indestructible logic that binds the Incarnation to the Atonement will be seen, and he who sees that neither statement has substance or efficacy apart from the other will have miraculously but solidly built that bridge which spans a gulf often threatening to separate the here and now from the there and then.[32]

The Relation between Christology and Soteriology

We have suggested that the principle of the relation between these two themes provides a benchmark for an adequate atonement theology. They are already related in the Nicene Creed, ("who for us men and our salvation") and have been present, at least implicitly throughout the history of

---

30. Maddox, *Responsible Grace*, 23; Lindström, *Wesley and Sanctification* concurs with this evaluation.

31. Cf. for example Hendry, *The Gospel of the Incarnation*.

32. Little, "Christ for Us and In Us." Little is responding to Rudolf Bultmann's existential interpretation of the Christian faith that disparages the historical in favor of present experience.

Christian thought. W. Pannenberg points out that every Christological theory is dominated by a soteriological concern.[33] Maddox argues that despite what the typical structure of Scholastic-influenced textbooks suggests, most theological traditions define the nature of Christ in light of what they consider to be the central benefits of the work of Christ. This was especially the case in the early debates over Christ's nature. Varying understandings of Christ emerged from differing conceptions of the basic human need and Christ's role in meeting that need.[34]

A survey of the history of theology reveals that at least four major types of atonement theory may be identified. I have listed some representative figures for each type. In a few cases, the classification may occasion surprise:

Exemplarist
Justin Martyr
Origen
Abelard (but see below)
Schleiermacher
Grotius' Governmental view

Transformational
Irenaeus
Athanasius
Eastern Church generally

Transactional
Anselm
Luther & Calvin
Evangelical Protestants generally

Representational
Ransom Theory
John McLeod Campbell
Gustav Aulén
Vincent Taylor

I need to say one further introductory word. It is clear that how one views the work of Christ is, or should be, logically related to one's understanding of several theological topics: the nature of God; the meaning of sin; the human predicament; and the significance of salvation. Each theory that has been advanced either presupposes or implies a particular understanding of each of these. My purpose is to seek to identify these presuppositions and offer a paradigm that is consistent with the whole tenor of Scripture and incorporates the whole Christ into a personal-relational paradigm that speaks a redemptive word to the whole need of the whole world.

---

33. Pannenberg, *Jesus—God and Man*, 39.
34. Maddox, *Responsible Grace*, 95.

2

Formation of the Eastern Perspective

It is often said that there was no theory of the atonement until Anselm (1098). Based on this misconception many subsequent thinkers read the Anselmian type of interpretation back into the New Testament and attempt to find anticipations of it in the early fathers. Actually, the major focus during the early Patristic period was upon the incarnation as addressing the perceived need of overcoming death or gaining immortality (life). To some extent one could say of the major Eastern fathers that the incarnation was the atonement.

In this chapter we propose to survey some representative figures of the Eastern (Greek) church to demonstrate this observation emphasizing their concern for the transformation of human nature (sanctification), and conclude with a brief analysis of one of the most significant theological principles of Eastern christology. There were also some other emphases present among these representatives that have re-emerged in contemporary theology.

Origen

Origen is considered the first scientific biblical scholar, but was probably more influenced by Greek thought than any other patristic scholar. Consistent with this influence he tended to view Christ's work as illumination. Reinhold Seeberg says: "If we inquire for the work of Christ [in Origen], we find the dominant thought to be, that Christ was physician, teacher, lawgiver, and example."[1]

But Adolf Harnack claimed that "his real originality lay in his combination of propitiation and literal ransom, of the expiatory sacrifice with the Marcionite notion of payment to the devil." He deemed the introduction of these two elements of "epoch-making proportions."[2] In commenting on Romans 3:25, Origen said that the Apostle "adds something more sublime,

---

1. Seeburg, *Text-Book of the History of Doctrines*, 153.
2. Franks, *The Work of Christ*, 41.

and declares that God set him forth a propitiation, by which, indeed, he would *make God propitious* to men by offering of his own body." However, these are mutually exclusive concepts. A death that is offered to the devil in payment of his claim cannot be at the same time an offering to God of a propitiatory sacrifice.

With regard to the first theme, Origen was the first to give status and currency to the idea that the devil had a rightful claim upon us, which could not be justly overlooked. He says:

> If therefore we were bought with a price, . . . we were bought doubtless from someone whose slaves we were, and who demanded such a price as he pleased for the release of those whom he held. It was the devil, however, who held us, to whom we had been allotted (or into whose power we had been dragged) by our sins. He therefore demanded as our price the blood of Christ.[3]

His idea of God's intentional deception of the devil was also adopted from the Gnostics. This view retained considerable currency until the time of Anselm.

Irenaeus

Irenaeus was one of the most prolific and careful theologians of the patristic period. His major work (*Against Heresies*) was primarily directed against the Gnostic speculations that threatened the integrity of the Christian faith. But in this lengthy treatise he developed two major, but interrelated, interpretations of the work of Christ distinctive of the Eastern mind.[4] Both of these involve primary focus on the incarnation. It was the fullest and most systematic development up to that time.

Irenaeus' interpretation of humanity as created in the image and likeness of God was central to his views. He derived this distinction from Genesis 1:26, failing to recognize that it was a Hebrew synonymous parallelism. Nonetheless it informed Christian thinking in the West about human nature until the Reformation and continues to shape Eastern thought. He interpreted the image as rationality, freedom, and responsibility. The likeness was eternal life, understood as sharing the divine nature, a gift of grace.

The likeness was lost in the fall through misuse of the gift of freedom with a two-fold result: 1) mankind became subject to death, and

---

3. Quoted. Ibid., 40.
4. Dunning, "The Concept of Original Sin."

2) also became captive to Satan. This meant that he was unable to fulfill his own nature, and being in captivity, was unable to free himself. Irenaeus seems to be the first Christian theologian to make critical use of the image of God concept and of human inability, which later came to be termed original sin.

Irenaeus understood God's redemptive action to involve the beginning of a new race *in Christ* as an alternative to the old race as described by the New Testament metaphor, *in Adam*. In bringing about this result, Christ did two things: 1) he broke the power of Satan and 2) restored humanity to eternal life. It may be said that the latter is the goal of God's redemptive action in Christ, whereas the former is the means.

This provides the rationale for the incarnation as being the atonement, which Irenaeus elaborates by his celebrated *Recapitulation* theory, derived biblically from Eph 1:10 where Paul states the eternal purpose of God to be to "gather up [sum up] all things in him, things in heaven and things on earth"[5] [NRSV]. Irenaeus own words nicely summarize his teaching: "But he was incarnate and made Man; and then he summed up in himself the long line of the human race, procuring for us a comprehensive salvation, that we might recover in Christ Jesus what in Adam we had lost, namely, the state of being in the image and likeness of God."[6]

Irenaeus' rationale is that since the fall came about by disobedience, restoration must occur through obedience. In accomplishing the necessary obedience, he insisted on what the later creeds affirmed about the incarnate one as being fully man and fully God. Irenaeus asks against the Ebionites, "How can they be saved unless he was God who wrought their salvation on the earth?" On the other hand he declares, "Had he not as man overcome man's adversary, the enemy would not have been justly overcome." In carrying out this task, Christ

> passed through every stage of life, restoring to each age fellowship with God . . . For as through the disobedience of one man, who was the first man, fashioned out of virgin soil, many were made sinners; so it was necessary that through the obedience of one man, who was the first to be born of a virgin, many should be justified and receive salvation." (iii.xvii.6–7)

The goal of redemption is captured in the classic phrase, "Our Lord Jesus Christ, the word of God, of his boundless love, became what we

---

5. Subsequent scripture references from New Revised Standard Version unless designated otherwise.

6. *Against Heresies*, III.xviii.1. Subsequent references to this source in text.

are that he might make us what he himself is." Typical of much Eastern thought, Irenaeus understood the consequence of the fall to be death. Since only God possessed immortality, it would seem that for humanity to regain the immortality lost in the fall, humans must become divine. Hence the goal of redemption has been described by the term *divination*. In Irenaeus' words, "And, if man had not been united to God, man could not have become a partaker of immortality." Hence it was in the incarnation, the union of deity with humanity, that the human was deified.

The standard liberal criticism of Irenaeus (following the interpretation of Adolf von Harnack) accused him of promoting a physical redemption. But in fact, he avoids using the term deification although other language seems to suggest the same idea. That is, he is accused of describing redemption in metaphysical or ontological categories rather than moral or purely religious terms. If this accusation was accurate, redemption would be both automatic and complete in the event of the incarnation with the cross having little or no significance. But several aspects of Irenaeus' teaching delegitimate this interpretation.

First is Irenaeus' emphasis on human faith in order for salvation to be personally appropriated; unbelief precludes man's participation in the salvation provided for him by the work of Christ. The converse of this was his emphasis on man's standing before God as a moral agent along with the consequences of sin for his relation to God. "According to nature," he wrote, "we are all sons of God, because we have all been created by God. But with respect to obedience and doctrine we are not all sons of God: those only are so who believe in him and do his will" (iv.xli.2). This statement illustrates the fact that his discussions of redemption are cast in relational language.

Actually he sees the result of sin to have affected both man's relation to God and his state of being. Thus redemption must address both and to do this Irenaeus points us to the entire life of Jesus, culminating in his death and resurrection. And to accomplish this full redemption, as we have noted, Jesus must be both God and man.

Trevor Hart, in a defense of Irenaeus against the liberal critique, says:

> Throughout the *Adversus haereses* the language of immortality and incorruptibility is inseparable from the language of atonement and reconciliation. To use Harnack's terms, the physical and the ethical fall together. For Irenaeus it would seem to be the case that what man *is* (his essence or nature) is not considered in a static manner, but is bound up with his relationships, and more particularly with his relationship to his Creator. Man's *being* is changed, therefore,

precisely because and insofar as his relationship with the Father is healed and renewed, and not in any mechanistic fashion.[7]

In sum, like Wesley (and St. Paul as well), the primary emphasis of Irenaeus on salvation is therapeutic in nature. God's redemptive purpose is ultimately to restore fallen humanity to the image and likeness of God.

Athanasius

Athanasius is probably best known as the defender of Nicene orthodoxy against Arianism. But the primary motivation for this concern was soteriological. Of the incarnation he says in his classic treatise: "He has yet been manifested to us in a human body for our salvation out of the loving-kindness and goodness of His own Father."[8]

He develops his rationale for the incarnation in the context of creation. Consequently he begins his argument with a discussion of the creation and the Creator "in order that one may duly recognize that its re-creation has been wrought by the Word who originally made it." The purposefulness of the creation is argued on the basis of the presence of design against those who posit chance; and the strength of God is defended on the basis of *creatio ex nihilo*. Furthermore the goodness of God reflects itself in a good creation, including mankind.

Logically, then, if the original creation was good, we must speak of a fall in order to explain the reason for the incarnation. The issue of the fall was death. This is related to the metaphysical assumption that evil is not-being, and good is being (chapter 4). The opposite of death is life, of mortality is immortality, and of corruption is incorruption. But since these qualities belong to God alone, and by nature man is mortal, man can only possess them by becoming divine. He quotes Psalm 82:6 in support of this position: "I say, 'You are gods, children of the Most High, all of you; nevertheless, you shall die like mortals, and fall like any prince.'" This text, along with 2 Peter 1:4, became standard proof texts for the Eastern teaching on divination. The first man possessed the qualities of life and immortality by a superadded gift of grace, which was forfeited in the fall.

Why did God not leave humankind in this predicament? Athanasius answers, "It was impossible, therefore, to leave man to be carried off by corruption, because it would be unfitting and unworthy of *God's goodness*" (59, emphasis added). Notice the basis of his argument from unfitting-

---

7. Hart, "Irenaeus, Recapitulation and Physical Redemption," 166.
8. Athanasius, *De Incarnatione Verbe Dei*, ch. 1. Subsequent references imbedded in text.

ness. We shall encounter a similar argument in Anselm but derived from a different understanding of the divine nature.

A very important consideration for Athanasius and significant for the purpose of this study is his contention that this restoration can only occur through transformation, thus forgiveness of sins is insufficient. Once again, basing his understanding of redemption on the divine nature, he denies that repentance will suffice:

> But repentance could not guard the consistency of God's character; for He would still remain untrue, if death did not hold the mastery over men. Nor does repentance recall men from what is according to their nature, but only makes them cease from their sins. If, indeed, it had only been a trespass, and not a consequent corruption, repentance would be well enough. But when once transgression gained a start, men came under the power of the corruption which was their nature, and were bereft of the grace which was theirs in virtue of their being made after God's image. What else were necessary to be done, or what was need for such grace and recall, but the Word of God, who also in the beginning had made everything out of nothing? (60)

This redemptive goal then provides the necessity for the incarnation of the Word who was fully God, thus possessing all the qualities that were lost in the fall and restoring them by uniting with human nature. Athanasius insists that this requires a real incarnation, not a theophany: "He did not will simply to become embodied, or merely to appear; for He might, if He willed simply to appear, as well have made His Divine Manifestation through some other and more excellent method: but He took our body, . . ."(61).

It furthermore requires a real death followed by a resurrection so that by truly dying and being raised from the dead he overcame death and restored life to all who identify with him. He illustrates this point with an analogy of an emperor who comes to dwell in a city:

> . . . Such city is naturally deemed worthy of much honour, and no enemy or bandit any longer descends upon it to overthrow it, but rather it is deemed worthy of all respect because of the emperor dwelling in one house there; so, too, is it with the Monarch of all. For all died; and He died for all, that we should no longer live unto ourselves, but unto Him who for our sakes died and rose from the dead. (63–64)

We can see the implications regarding the consequences for humanity of the incarnation even if we may question a bit of naïveté in the analogy.

He includes in his rationale also the idea that in his incarnation, death and resurrection the Word overcame the devil. This conquest is interpreted in terms of his central view of the human predicament being death: "He also Himself in like manner partook of the same; that through death He might bring to naught him that had the power of death, that is, the devil; and might deliver all those who through fear of death were all their lifetime subject to bondage" (65).

Another aspect—and very important for understanding the enduring significance of this way of viewing soteriology—is his emphasis on the image of God. Lost in the fall, the *imago* was re-embodied in the incarnation of the Word, and designed to be restored to the human race. Here, the incarnation performs a revelatory function. He describes this in a lovely analogy: "For as, when a portrait painted on a panel has disappeared in consequence of external stains, there is need again for him to come whose the portrait is, that the likeness may be renewed on the same material; but the likeness is retraced upon it; . . ." (73). The latter part of this analogy has implications for the nature of the human. There is no need for a new creation *ex nihilo* since the essentially human does not need to be replaced but restored.

Athanasius own words well sums up the two-fold benefit of the incarnation: "For the Saviour, through His incarnation, in his loving-kindness effected both these things: He made death to vanish from us, and renewed us; . . ." (78).

If the problematic for Irenaeus was Jesus' humanity (called into question by Gnosticism), for Athanasius it was his deity. This, he argues, Jesus established via his miracles, especially the exorcisms (82). He then summarizes his position:

> But since what was due from all must needs be paid—for it was due that all should die, as I said before—for this reason specially He dwelt among us: to this end, after the proofs of His Godhead from His works, He then offered up the sacrifice also on behalf of all, surrendering His own temple to death in place of all, to make all men no more liable to the account, and free from the old transgression; and to show Himself also mightier than death, showing forth His own body incorruptible as first fruits of the resurrection of all. (85)

This summary contains the statement that captures Athanasius' rationale concerning the necessity for the death of Christ: "it was due that all should die." But only the God-man could suffer a redeeming death since he alone is not subject to death (86). Therefore it must be demonstrated to be both voluntary and real and be succeeded by the resurrection so that those who are identified with him could be free from the punishment of death.

This brief survey, particularly of Irenaeus and Athanasius, demonstrates that the Greek fathers of this period generally conceived of sin as a disease or corruption of human nature, which was potentially cured by Christ's incorporation of mankind in himself, and actualized by our identification with him.

One consideration remains, to explore the significance of a principle declared by several but most centrally articulated by one of the Cappadocian Fathers, Gregory of Nazianzen:

> The unassumed is the unhealed; however, that which is united to his Godhead is saved. If only half of Adam fell, then Christ assumes and saves only that half of his nature. But if his nature fell in its totality, then it must all be united to the nature of him who was begotten, and thus be saved in its totality. Let them not begrudge us our salvation in its totality, or clothe the savior with nothing more than bones and nerves and something which looks like humanity.[9]

It was this soteriological principle that served as the bulwark against the Apollinarian heresy, which declared the volitional aspect of the divine-human person to have been taken by the Logos. This explanation of the incarnation implied that he was not *fully* human. The soteriological implications of Gregory's formula have been widely criticized, failing to recognize the complexities of its implications.[10] In a word, the prevailing critique of this so-called realist theory of redemption fails to recognize the significance of the position as articulated by Irenaeus and Athanasius.

In a masterful defense of the cogency of this formula, T. J. Gorringe points out four ways in which the common critique fails to do justice to its soteriological significance.

First, for both Irenaeus and Athanasius, God's act in Christ is part of a *process* of redemption, a process in which the incarnation is the decisive moment, but which is continued *post Christum* by God's work as Spirit. The presupposition behind this is another distinctive feature of Eastern

---

9. Quoted in McGrath, *Christian Theology*, 289.
10. Kelly, *Early Christian Doctrines*, 111.

theology: human beings were not created perfect but with a potentiality for perfection.

This assumption informed Irenaeus' distinction between the image and likeness. The former is that which constitutes humanness while the latter is spiritual in nature. Though created in the image, the first pair were to grow in increasing conformity to the likeness. But sin entered the picture thus aborting this teleological existence. While the incarnation would have occurred if there had been no fall, its particular form and function were necessitated by this disruption.

Thus, as the second Adam, Jesus recapitulated the divine intention, achieving the perfection of full conformity to the image by a lifetime of obedience to the Father. He thereby undid what Adam did. By our faith union with him we are called to a life-long pursuit of holiness. Through him we may become "partakers of the Divine nature" (2 Pet 1:4).

Second, the moral dimension of redemption is really more important than the critics allow. Athanasius, in particular, emphasizes that humanity's turn toward corruption was a moral turn with physical consequences, and the work of Christ is for "turning them again toward incorruption." The abolition of death and corruption (understood as mortality) is interpreted as the necessary presupposition for the full renewing of the image of God in humankind and this occurs *physically* at the consummation of the process. Thus *deification* is a way of talking about the work of grace renewing the image in us, renewing us by bringing us into communion with God.

Third is the whole understanding of redemption as a work of divine pedagogy of those oppressed by corruption. In a later work than the one we have explored, Athanasius speaks of the purpose of the incarnation as being that "sin might be completely expelled from the flesh and that we might have a free mind" (*Contr. Ar.* I.56).

Fourth, is the theme of the struggle against evil. As Gorringe summarizes:

> When Irenaeus or Athanasius, therefore, argue that "not assumed is not healed," they understand the incarnation, God taking human flesh and mind, as standing at the center of a process of divine pedagogy which is at the same time a battle with the powers that corrupt and ruin human nature, a battle joined in creation and continued in the Spirit. This ongoing process must be understood when the formula is read.[11]

---

11. Gorringe, "'Not Assumed Is Not Healed,'" 481–90.

3

Development of the Western Tradition

To the Cappadocians and Alexandrians, the incarnation was a splendid end in itself. To the Latin thinkers it became more and more a means to an end. The God-man was not a bond uniting God and man, manifesting their essential likeness and kinship, but a witness of their disunity and a means of creating union. They laid great stress on the sufferings and death of Christ, but until Anselm these emphases were not turned into an articulated theory of the atonement.

How do we explain the dramatic difference between the East and West? While it may be overly simple, at least one dominant reason (if not the most significant one) is the presence of a mindset indigenous to Western civilization derived from a preoccupation with law and juridical matters. This mindset became native to western Christendom to a great extent through the influence of a second century father named Tertullian whose impact on Western theology has been very pervasive. We begin our study by looking at this man and the assumptions he introduced into the theology of the West.

Tertullian

It is impossible to over-emphasize the importance of Tertullian for the development of Christian theology. His views on the trinity, christology and soteriology became normative for the Western church. Since Tertullian became a heretic because of his fiery zeal and rigorous Christian teachings, joining the Montanists out of reaction to the growing worldliness of the church, his influence was mediated through Cyprian, who was the architect of Western ecclesiology, and Augustine, whose views were shaped by Tertullian's thought-forms. Most important for our purposes was the fact that he cast Western Christian thought in a legal mode.[1]

Tertullian was evidently a jurist although he does not explicitly state that this was his educational background and some recent scholars have

---

1. Gonzalez, *Christian Thought Revisited*, 20–22, 50–52. Cf. also Aulén, *Christus Victor*.

called this into question. But the following information from Eusebius is rather definitive. He tells us that Tertullian was possibly destined for state official life and was celebrated for his knowledge of Roman law. He adds that Tertullian was a "man well versed in the laws of the Romans, and in other respects of high repute, and one of those especially distinguished in Rome."[2]

As a jurist (or one profoundly impacted by legal modes of thought), Tertullian regarded the relation of humanity to God from that point of view. God was understood as the lawgiver and the avenger of transgressions of the law. Thus the fundamental relation of mankind to God is that of fear.

The sinner can find salvation by repentance whereby he earns for himself salvation in baptism. He says, "[God] offers impunity to be purchased by this compensation of repentance." Note the commercial transaction flavor of this. In this teaching, baptism assumes a fixed position in the order of salvation since the grace of God is necessarily connected to this sacrament. By baptism, guilt and punishment are removed "death having been destroyed through the washing away of sins, and the guilt thus removed, punishment is also removed."

In this context, Tertullian introduced the term *satisfaction* into the theological vocabulary of the West, a term he derived from Roman law. After having received baptismal grace, we may remain therein if we do not sin, but fulfill the law of God. If we sin, we offend God and, as Tertullian says, "if he is offended, he ought to be angry." Satisfaction must now be rendered in view of this wrath of God. Note that for him satisfaction is for post-baptismal sins.

Tertullian also introduces, in substance, the distinction between mortal and venial sin. This distinction came to inform the concept of purgatory, which was developed later. Venial sin will prolong your stay in purgatory but will not damn you eternally in hell. One who commits mortal sin will be eternally lost.

Here are the raw materials that resulted in the development of the sacrament of penance, which officially became a Roman Catholic sacrament in 1439. There were initially four steps in the sacrament: contrition, confession, satisfaction, and absolution. Contrition meant that you were sorry that you had sinned. You confess to the priest who determines what you should do to render satisfaction to God. After this, he pronounces the word of absolution: "I absolve you of guilt." These elements were later changed to attrition, confession, absolution, and satisfaction. On the as-

---

2. Quoted in Morgan, *The Importance of Tertullian*, 5.

sumption that contrition was not possible to one in sin, it was changed from being sorry that you sinned (contrition) to being sorry you got caught (attrition). The order of the last two was reversed and the word of absolution was pronounced after which you were to render satisfaction. It becomes something like having to do work for which you have already been paid. As Reinhold Seeburg says, "In the attempt to make repentance difficult, it is made easy. For that which is the hardest thing in religion—repentance and faith—is substituted good works."[3]

The entire moral life is thus regarded from a legal point of view. Man is to fulfill the law—not only its precepts but, if possible, also its counsels of perfection, an idea derived from Jesus' words to the rich, young ruler. Thereby one becomes holy and righteous and recompenses Christ for his redeeming work. In a word, good works are meritorious.

If one does more than is necessary for salvation, he acquires surplus merit. Tertullian says: "Good done has God as debtor, just as has evil also, because the Judge is a rewarder of every case." This flowers in the concept of the *Treasury of Merit* that became the occasion for Martin Luther's posting his 95 theses, which in turn precipitated the controversies resulting in the Protestant Reformation.

The concept of merit introduced by Tertullian into the Western view of the Christian life continued to be normative for that branch of Christendom, not only in Roman Catholic theology but also, as we shall see, in much Protestant theology as well.[4]

Thus for Tertullian salvation was composed of sacraments and laws. While he did not develop these concepts into a theory of the atonement, the groundwork for such was laid by Cyprian and they came to fruition in the work of Anselm.

Anselm's *Cur Deus Homo*

Anselm is one of the most important theologians of the Middle Ages. He lived during a time when many scholars had great confidence in human reason and theologized from the implicit assumption that reason can apprehend the essence of God. This optimism is the presupposition that informed Anselm's famous ontological argument for the existence of God. It proceeded on the premise that God's essence included his existence and since reason could perceive the essence of God, to deny his existence would

---

3. Seeburg, *History of Doctrines*, 197.

4. See discussion in Richardson, *Theology of the New Testament*, 239–40. Richardson comments: "Merit is a notion which the NT entirely discards."

be a contradiction in terms, something like denying that all bachelors are unmarried men. This optimism was soon called into question by a much more influential theologian, Thomas Aquinas, and even more radically by Duns Scotus and William of Occam. It was this optimistic rationalism that also informed Anselm's analysis of the atonement.

However, to be fair to Anselm, we must recognize that he understood his methodology to be embodied in the formula *fides quarens intellectum,* (faith seeking understanding). In other words, if this applies to his *Cur Deus Homo*, he would understand himself to be using reason to better understand what he accepts by faith. That would imply that the basic concepts were already present in the prevailing theological thinking of his culture. With these preliminary notes, we proceed to an analysis of the arguments by which Anselm seeks to answer the question, "why the God-man?"

Exposition of *Cur Deus Homo*

He states the question embodied in the title succinctly in the opening pages of the work, which appears to have an apologetic purpose and clearly reflects his optimism that Christian truth can be demonstrated by reason:

> And this question, both infidels are accustomed to bring up against us, ridiculing Christian simplicity as absurd; and many believers ponder it in their hearts; for what cause or necessity, in sooth, God became man, and by his own death, as we believe and affirm, restored life to the world; when he might have done this, by means of some other being, angelic or human, or merely by his will.[5]

The point at issue concerns the means of achieving the goal of salvation. The arguments addressing this matter revolve around the concepts of "fitting," "unfitting," and "necessity." The relation of "fitting" and "unfitting" is parallel to the relation between possible and impossible.[6] Anselm illustrates fittingness in this way:

> For, as death came upon the human race by the disobedience of man, it was *fitting* that by man's obedience life should be restored. And, as sin, the cause of our condemnation, had its origin from a woman, so ought the author of our righteousness and salvation to be born of a woman. And so also was it proper that the devil, who,

---

5. Anselm, *Cur Deus Homo*, 192–93. Subsequent references to this work will be inserted in the text in parentheses.

6. The following analysis of Anselm's argument is heavily dependent upon the insights of Root, "Necessity and Unfittingness in Anselm's *Cur Deus Homo*," 211–30.

being man's tempter, and conquered him in eating of the tree, should be vanquished by man in the suffering of the tree which man bore. (197, emphasis added)

But Anselm's dialog partner, Boso, points out that this does not constitute a necessity, that is, irrefutable proof to the infidels even though what Anselm describes is beautiful. What is required, insists Boso, is to show "the rational existence of the truth, I mean, the necessity, which proves that God ought to or could have condescended to those things which we affirm" (198). Some instances appear to equate fittingness with necessity, as when Anselm summarizes the argument that will be spelled out in the rest of the treatise:

> Does not the reason why God ought to do the things we speak of seem absolute enough when we consider that the human race, that work of his so very precious, was wholly ruined, and that it was not seemly that the purpose which God had made concerning man should fall to the ground; and moreover, that this purpose could not be carried into effect unless the human race were delivered by their Creator himself. (198)

This sounds a lot like Athanasius, as we previously noted, but as the argument proceeds it will become clear that it is quite different, being developed on other presuppositions about the divine nature than those which informed the Eastern theologian's work.

The question to be explored is how can Anselm move from fittingness to necessity. Ultimately he actually argues from *unfittingness* to necessity. This is the key to his argument.

The first step in the argument develops the assertion that the goal or end for which God created the world *must* be achieved. The two-fold end is *order* in the universe and *rectitude* or justice for rational creatures. Both are seen in relation to God. Early on Anselm says,

> it is moreover shown by plain reasoning and fact that human nature was ordained for this purpose, viz., that every man should enjoy a happy immortality, both in body and in soul; and that it was necessary that this design for which man was made should be fulfilled; but that it could not be fulfilled unless God became man, and unless all things were to take place which we hold with regard to Christ. (191–92)

Will humanity achieve this end? The answer lies not in human ability but in the nature of God. Can the divine intention fail? The answer is a resounding *no!* ". . . It will follow that God either could not accomplish the good which he begun [sic], or he will repent of having undertaken it; either of which is absurd" (237). This same affirmation is made with equal vigor late in the treatise in a statement that also reflects Anselm's high view of human reason: "Now if it be understood that God has made nothing more valuable than rational existence capable of enjoying him; it is altogether foreign from his character to suppose that he will suffer that rational existence utterly to perish" (256). Thus necessity resides in the divine nature, which cannot fail to accomplish his ultimate purpose. It is very interesting here that the *order* of the universe referred to above is seen in terms of the number of persons to be saved needing to correspond to the number of fallen angels in order to restore the original order of creation (224, 237), a theme derived from St. Augustine.

The second step in Anselm's argument is the demonstration that the incarnation and crucifixion of Christ are necessarily the means God uses to realize his original creative intent.

Since the path from God's original creative intent to its final realization was thwarted by the reality of sin, we need to ask, what is sin? It is here that Anselm's cultural situation clearly shapes his theological understanding. Sin is failing to give God his due (215–16).

Furthermore, the effects of sin are not limited to the individual or to humanity, it upsets the order of the universe and thus the universe no longer gives God the honor and praise it owes God and for which it was created. This introduces an element Anselm describes as "unseemliness springing from the violation of the beauty of arrangement." If this were not corrected, "God would appear to be deficient in his management" (224).

How will God respond? We can conclude with certainty (because it is necessary) that God will not simply abandon humanity. What God starts, God finishes. Once again, this sounds like Athanasius but argued on a different basis.

According to Anselm God has two options. He can either forgive out of mercy or demand repayment of the honor stolen from him (217). He quickly offers 3 reasons why the first is unfitting based on the principle that "to remit sin in this manner [simply forgive] is nothing else than not to punish; and since it is not right to cancel sin without compensation or punishment; if it be not punished, then is it passed by undischarged." Thus

1) "it is not fitting for God to pass over anything in his kingdom undischarged"
2) if sin is unpunished, "with God there will be no difference between the guilty and the not guilty; and this is unbecoming to God"; and

3) if sin is neither paid for nor punished, it is subject to no law. This last reason highlights the justice of God since, Anselm argues, "Everyone knows that justice to man is regulated by law, so that, according to the requirements of law, the measure of award is bestowed by God" (217–18).

This leads us to the culmination of this phase of the argument, which is simply stated

> Therefore, consider it settled that, without satisfaction, that is, without voluntary payment of the debt, God can neither pass by the sin unpunished, nor can the sinner attain that happiness, or happiness like that, which he had before he sinned; for man cannot in this way be restored, or become such as he was before he sinned. (238–39)

The restoration of the right order of creation and the elevation of humanity to its destined goal are so intertwined that the second is an inherent condition of the first. Since, Anselm believes, right order can only be restored by *satisfaction*, the question now arises, who can make satisfaction? Once again, rational argument comes to Anselm's aid. If a being other than God were to effect the satisfaction, and rescue man from eternal death, "man would rightly be adjudged as the servant of that being. But the order of the universe depended on man (and other rational beings) serving God and thus the goal could not be accomplished in this way" (198–99). The only logical conclusion is that God alone can make the satisfaction.

Yet humanity must make satisfaction or it would be unfitting. But this satisfaction must be made on the principle that the satisfaction has to be proportionate to guilt. Anselm argued that if this were not the case "sin would remain in a manner exempt from control [unordered], which cannot be, for God leaves nothing uncontrolled [unordered] in his kingdom. But this is determined, that even the smallest unfitness is impossible with God" (239–40). In fact, Anselm further affirms that the required satisfaction must "restore something greater than the amount of that obligation," in order to serve as a deterrent to further sin (244).

Boso is abashed by the argument because the requirements seem to leave no way of salvation (250). But this is where all the parts of the argument come together. Since a human *must* pay the debt and only God *can* pay it, "it is necessary for the God-man to [pay] it" (259).

How does the God–man make satisfaction? As a rational creature he already owes complete obedience to God's will. As sinless, however, he does not owe to God his death. The one adequate satisfaction is then the laying down his life for the honor of God (269–72) Q.E.D.

An important question to put to this tightly reasoned logical argument is, for whom does He make satisfaction? The answer, which really turns out to be somewhat ambiguous, revolves around the concept of merit, although that particular term is not used. Other terms such as *reward* and *possessions* are used as synonyms. Since the God-man owed nothing to God, what he did earned a reward commensurate with who he was, namely surplus merit. Since he did not need it, he could will it to be given to another. But to whom? Boso joyfully exclaims, "it seems to me that God can reject none who come to him in his [the God-man's] name" (297f.). Although, the logic that has informed the treatise thoughout is abandoned, it appears that Anselm wishes the provision of the Atonement to be universal in its scope.

On this point George Hendry highlights what he calls a "manifest equivocation in the argument."

> The justice that gives a man [Jesus] freedom to dispose of his own as he may choose is of a different kind from the justice that Anselm invokes at an earlier stage to support the argument that the unconditional remission of sins by God would be an irregularity [*Cur Deus Homo*, II.19]. The Son enjoys a range of freedom that is denied the Father; yet since the Father both instigates and approves the action of the Son, he countenances an irregularity, though himself incapable of it. It is only the appearance of justice that is preserved by means of a legal artifice.[7]

Anselm's view is typically Latin, influenced by the legal mentality of the Roman mind and the prevailing view of law. Sin was conceived as a debt, and penance was regarded as compensation, the quantitative element making commutation possible. If certain acts were the legal *equivalents* of certain sins, one kind of penance could be bartered or substituted for another kind. As the equivalence was arbitrary, the church soon came to appropriate grace on easier conditions. The next step was the commutation of a penitential act by the payment of money; after that the descent into the circumstances that were major factors in the Reformation debate was easy.

The alternatives that Anselm envisions were consistent with both Roman and German law of the time: either punishment or satisfaction.

---

7. Hendry, *The Gospel of the Incarnation*, 120.

Gustav Aulén argues that these ideas were really derived from the concept of penance.[8]

Feudalism provided the form of the theory since sin was conceived as injuring the honor of God with the resulting need for compensation. So from feudalism came the following features:

    1) God's relates to man as a feudal lord to a serf;

    2) sin involves the loss of God's honor;

    3) Christ's obedience (as man) is seen as a service; and

    4) Christ's service is a substitute for ours.[9]

This theory has sometimes been referred to as the "commercial theory"; the "mathematical theory" (idea of equivalence); and (as above) the "feudal theory," based on the idea of medieval chivalry. Anselm's reduction of the work of Christ to formal, exact syllogisms is in complete contrast to the varied, metaphorical, unsystematic method of the New Testament. His primary concern is how to escape punishment. And his solution is based on what he repeatedly refers to as the fitness and unfitness of things.

It should be noted that what is fitting or unfitting is a subjective judgment depending on the values of the one who does the judging. Thus one who approaches the issues from a different perspective may have a much different view of what is fitting or unfitting. If Anselm would argue that his view is derived from the nature of God as taught in scripture, then we must radically disagree.

The chief merit of Anselm's theory is that it dealt a death-blow to the ancient notion that man was the devil's lawful prey, and that the slaveholder's claims must be met before the ransom is complete. This resulted in a practical value in that it delivered the medieval world from the unnatural dread of God that the church was engendering. In spite of some appearances to the contrary, it made the thought of God more alluring than the prevailing concept. *We* do not have to appease God; it is done on our behalf. And God *will* accept satisfaction.

But it has some serious defects. As George Hendry says, "It is inconsistent with the New Testament, which uniformly represents the atonement as a movement, of which God is not only the originator but the active agent, and which he directs toward man."[10]

---

    8. Aulén, *Christus Victor*, 82.

    9. Foley, *Anselm's Theory of the Atonement*. Green and Baker, *Recovering the Scandal of the Cross*, suggest that the value of Anselm's formulation is in its relevance to the prevailing cultural situation, but which is neither Biblical nor contemporary, 126–36.

    10. Hendry, *The Gospel of the Incarnation*, 117.

Abelard

In addition to the elements in the tradition of the church picked up and developed by Anselm, there was also the conception that Christ appeared to reveal the love of God, which by teaching and example leads to responsive love and piety. In reaction to the emphases of Anselm, this aspect was stressed by Abelard.

He did agree with Anselm in rejecting the idea of meeting the claims of the devil as having no just right to humanity. Based on his observation that God could (and did) forgive sins before the death of Christ he rejected the Anselmian necessity of the death as a satisfaction. Also, he argued that it was improper that the blood of the innocent should be demanded as a ransom. God is not reconciled, does not need to be reconciled, by the death of his Son.

Abelard's Positive Statement

Through the works of the law no one could become righteous. But in Christ the love of God was made manifest in that he assumed our nature and, as our teacher and example, remained faithful unto death. This love admonishes us to an answering love toward God and awakens it in us. By virtue of our faith in the love of God made manifest in Christ, we are united with Christ, as with our neighbor, by an indissoluble bond of love. The love thus awakened in our hearts is the ground of the forgiveness of sins, according to Luke 7:47. Thus we are redeemed from sin and from fear, since Christ works love in us.

But Abelard did not fully escape the idea of merit. Christ, in becoming man, subjected himself to the commandment of love for others. This law he fulfilled "both by instructing us and by praying for us." It is in this way, since his prayers must on account of his righteousness be heard, that Christ "supplements from his merits what was lacking in ours."[11]

Abelard was opposed in his own day for failing to recognize the central place of the cross or the need for regeneration. He is accused of having an overly optimistic view of human nature and a less serious view of the effect of the fall on human ability.[12]

---

11. Cf. Taylor, "Was Abelard an Exemplarist?" 207–13.

12. Bernard of Clairvaux charged Abelard with teaching that Christ lived and died "for no other purpose than that he might teach us how to live by his words and example, and point out, by his passion and death, to what limits our love should go. Thus he did not communicate righteousness, but only revealed to us what it is." Quoted in McGrath, "The Moral Theory of the Atonement," 205–20.

In contrast to the near universal interpretation of Abelard's position, Alister McGrath argues that he was actually not an exemplarist but that this widespread misunderstanding resulted from the isolation of a single, small portion of his exposition of Romans as representative of his position as a whole. Rather, says McGrath, he is an "exemplarist if, and only if, it can be shown that he understands Christ to be our example, *through whose imitation we are redeemed*—whereas it is clear that he understands Christ to be our example in the sense, that *because we are redeemed by him*, we now wish to imitate him."[13]

If the moral influence theory is understood in this way, Colin Williams' argument that John Wesley draws the moral influence theory into his theology in relation to his picture of the Christian life puts Wesley in Abelard's camp.[14]

McGrath's contention is that the popularity of the exemplarist theory in the liberal period of the twentieth century was the result of the rejection of a number of aspects of orthodox theology, and attributes much of its popularity to the work of Hastings Rashdall who misunderstood Abelard.

Nevertheless the two options represented by the transactional interpretation of Anselm and the exemplarist theory, even if not conclusively Abelard's, rather set the pattern for subsequent discussions in the West on the issues surrounding the understanding of the work of Christ. McGrath notwithstanding, the exemplarist interpretation is all but universally attributed to Abelard.

Thomas Aquinas

In his survey of the period between Anselm and Aquinas, Seeberg says, "The present period produced nothing new touching the work of Christ. The attempt was made . . . to combine the objective view, in which the ideas of Anselm were accepted, with Abelard's subjective interpretation . . . The noteworthy discussion of the subject by Thomas follows the same line."[15]

With Aquinas' work we reach the climax of the scholastic movement, the most complete and comprehensive expression of the Medieval Synthesis. His *Summa Theologica* is universally recognized as one of the classic works of Christian theology, exercising continuing influence, es-

---

13. Ibid.
14. Williams, *John Wesley's Theology Today*, 77–82.
15. Seeberg, *History of Doctrines*, 110–11.

pecially among Roman Catholic theologians. Unlike Abelard's *Sic et non* (Yes and No) that was designed to demonstrate that the church fathers did not speak with united voice, Thomas attempted to demonstrate that when placed in context, most of them were voicing at least one aspect of the truth.

But as Ronald Wallace said, "Thomas gave himself a difficult task," which resulted in Adolph Harnack's accusing him of "failing to convey any 'distinct impression.'"[16] But this does mean that he finds a way to support a wide variety of views ranging from Anselm to Abelard in the West and including as well certain aspects of the Eastern perspective.

Two presuppositions, one philosophical and the other theological, informed Thomas' reasoning about the work of Christ. Unlike Anselm, who was a thoroughgoing rationalist, Thomas was a moderate empiricist like his philosophical mentor, Aristotle. Believing that human reason had access to God's essential being, Anselm taught that God's action was subject to a logical necessity. Thomas, on the other hand, held that God's relation to the world and to all in it that is ordered by God is marked by contingency.[17] As applied to the atonement, this assumption led Thomas to reject Anselm's tightly reasoned argument seeking to affirm the necessity of God's honor being satisfied and affirmed instead that "it was not necessary in any other sense than that God willed to save men this way."[18]

The theological presupposition to which I referred relates to the order of salvation. His work is the sophisticated expression of the understanding that had become prevalent in Roman Catholic piety, namely that salvation or final acceptance by God was based upon one's holiness, or ethical righteousness. Thus the order of salvation was seen as originating in faith which basically meant belief in and acceptance of the authority of the teachings of the church. From that point on, the Christian life was characterized by the formula, "faith formed by love" (*fides formata caritas*). Based on Aristotle's analysis of causation, this meant that faith alone was insufficient but, like the seed planted in the ground, it must germinate, energized by the pull of the final form (perfect love) until it's potentiality has been fully actualized. This ultimate goal is also referred to as beatitude (happiness) constituted by the vision of the divine being.

In addition to his argument from human incapacity to apprehend the essence of God, Thomas offers another refutation of Anselm's concept

---

16. Wallace, *Atoning Death of Christ*, 75.

17. Thomas Aquinas, *Summa Theologica*, I.1.1. Subsequent references in text. Cf. Franks, *The Work of Christ*, 207.

18. Wallace, *The Atoning Death of Christ*, 75.

of necessity. Anselm had argued that God's justice demanded a necessary satisfaction for human sin and that God could not deny his own justice without denying himself. Thomas replies:

> This justice depends upon the will of God, demanding from the human race satisfaction for sin; for, if He had wished to deliver man from sin without any satisfaction, He would have done nothing contrary to justice: for the judge, who has to punish an offence committed against some other, as for instance some other man or the whole state, or the prince above him, cannot without violating justice remit the offence without punishment; but God has no other above Him, but He Himself is the supreme and common good of the universe. And therefore, if He remit sin, which comes under the category of an offence, because it is committed against Himself, He does no one wrong; just as any man, of his mercy, forgives without satisfaction, and does no wrong. (III.46.1)

Although Anselm had first defined satisfaction in accordance with the rule of private law, in order to demonstrate its necessity he had spoken of God as the moral ruler of the universe who cannot remit sin unpunished.[19] Thomas countered this by asserting that sin is a personal affront to God and that "the Divine Sovereign is to be interpreted according to the rule of private law." As Franks comments truly: "This is an immensely important position: as long as it remains uncontroverted, the Anselmic doctrine is vitiated at an essential point," and proceeds to observe that "it is just round about this point, however, that controversy rages in later attempts to apply legal analogies to the work of Christ."[20]

In our subsequent discussions we shall argue that it is precisely this issue that has been the source of the Western church's difficulty in coming to a sound, Biblical view of the work of Christ. In a word, as long as the issues are cast in a legal mode, rather than in terms of personal relations, we will find ourselves faced with inadequate theology.

Thomas develops his understanding of the passion of Christ in the context of his discussion of grace. There is a "first grace" which is unmerited and establishes one's relation to God. "The sinner then can never merit eternal life, except he first be reconciled to God by the forgiveness of sins, which takes place by grace."[21] Thus forgiveness takes place via the

---

19. Franks, *Work of Christ*, 220.
20. Ibid., 221.
21. Ibid., 212.

merit of Christ, although Thomas does allow the saints to merit this first grace for others.

The "second grace," as we might call it, is "cooperating grace" by which we are enabled to do good works and merit the full holiness that qualifies one for the beatific vision. It is this process that is described by the formula, "faith formed by love."

Here Thomas is following Aristotle's principle that men become good by doing good until goodness becomes habituated. In the Angelic Doctor's own words, "Men, however, obtain [beatitude] by many motions of operations, which are called merits, wherefore according to the Philosopher [Aristotle], beatitude is the reward of virtuous operations" (II.1.5, art. 7).

We may now proceed to a brief description of Thomas' interpretation of the work of Christ in the light of these presuppositions. It is true, his thinking continues to be informed by the ideas of merit and satisfaction but he has abandoned the Anselmic idea of necessity and says God has simply chosen this way because it is fitting. Furthermore, he sees the passion of Christ to include the entire Christ event.

We can do no better than quote Thomas' own statement on satisfaction, which is quite clear and free of scholastic jargon:

> I reply that a proper satisfaction comes about when someone offers to the person offended something which gives him a delight greater than his hatred of the offence. Now Christ by suffering as a result of love and obedience offered to God something greater than what might be exacted in compensation for the whole offence of humanity; firstly, because of the greatness of the love, as a result of which he suffered; secondly, because of the worth of the life which he laid down for a satisfaction, which was the life of God and of a human being; thirdly, because of the comprehensiveness of his passion and the greatness of the sorrow which he took upon himself . . . And therefore the passion of Christ was not only sufficient but a superabundant satisfaction for the sins of the human race. (IIIa.48.2)

On the basis of this passage Seeberg points out that, in addition to parting company with the juristic conception of Anselm, on account of the greatness of Christ's love and the value of his life whereby he offered a superabundant satisfaction, both the necessity and the equivalence of the satisfaction are surrendered.[22]

One additional note might be important as it reflects an understanding that militates against the central Biblical claim that "in Christ, God

---

22. Seeberg, *History of Doctrines*, 2:112.

was reconciling the world to himself" (2 Cor 5:19). Thomas taught that "Christ assumed not only bodily defects, but also defects of soul: in particular His soul was passible."[23] The fact that passibility or the capacity to suffer is seen as a defect means that the suffering of Christ was the function of his human nature and God could not actually participate in that suffering. In subsequent discussions we shall see that this understanding, derived from Greek philosophy, has been widely abandoned in more recent-and better-Biblical understanding thus opening the door to God's full involvement in the reconciling work of Christ.

Aquinas' balanced and moderating interpretation of the work of Christ provides a good resource for understanding the best of medieval theology. However, at the popular level where education was rare and superstition was rampant, the carefully nuanced ideas of Thomas became a highly objectionable popular piety. The exploitation of the fears generated by the whole complex of popular piety became the catalyst for the Protestant Reformation.

---

23. Franks, *Work of Christ*, 216–17.

4

The Atonement in Protestant Theology

OUR PURPOSE in this chapter is to demonstrate that, even though there were significant discontinuities between Roman Catholic theology and that of the classical Protestant Reformers, the same presuppositions regarding the work of Christ and the basis of salvation were present and this gave a unique form to their teaching. We shall look primarily at Martin Luther and John Calvin, the major Reformers, and then note how their basic principles were transformed (or perhaps distorted) into the Protestant Scholasticism or orthodoxy of the seventeenth century.

Martin Luther

Luther is obviously one of the most important figures in the history of theology, but also one of the more difficult to interpret because of the unsystematic character of his works. Based, no doubt, on these characteristics, Jim Siggins argues that: "Luther has no theory of the atonement."[1] But it does seem possible to identify three major motifs in his work: the *Christus Victor* theme, the substitutionary theme and the satisfaction theme in relation to the wrath of God.

Gustav Aulén has insisted that Luther's primary vision was the *Christus Victor* motif. He devotes an entire chapter to defending this thesis and argues that the other themes are all incorporated into this one.[2] But John T. Mueller takes issue with Aulén and affirms, along with many others, that Luther was no systematic theologian operating from a central norm in regard to this topic but rather availed himself of the plethora of Biblical metaphors feeling that they communicated the truth of the Gospel sufficiently for his audience. Mueller emphasized the continuity of Luther with Anselm on satisfaction but argues that Luther did "treat it

---

1. Siggins, *Martin Luther's Doctrine of Christ*.
2. Aulén, *Christus Victor*, 101–22.

primarily from God's love in Christ Jesus, so that his viewpoint is decidedly evangelical."[3]

Luther's own words appear to support Mueller:

> Then ascend higher through the heart of Christ to the heart of God, and see that Christ would not have been able to love you if God had not willed it in eternal love, to which Christ is obedient in his love toward you; there you will find the divine, good father heart, and, as Christ says, be thus drawn to the Father through Christ.[4]

This perspective was no doubt the corollary of his discovery of the Pauline use of the concept of the righteousness of God in Romans. The prevailing medieval theology had taught that the righteousness of God was the ethical righteousness that God required of humanity in order to become acceptable. One of the most dramatic and best known chapters in Christian history is young Luther's struggles with this understanding as he sought to find a gracious God. The great breakthrough in his own experience came with the discovery that, properly interpreted, it was God's own righteousness, his attitude of mercy and compassion toward the undeserving and unworthy that was the basis of his acceptance.

Mueller went on to argue that

> . . . Christ's merit and satisfaction are central in [Luther's] evangelical theology. Essentially, therefore, there is no difference between Luther and Anselm in their teaching of Christ's atoning work. Both use the same terms emphasizing the propitiatory and objective character of the atonement. Practically the only real difference between Luther and Anselm is that the Wittenburg reformer stressed also the active obedience of Christ, or his vicarious fulfillment of the divine law, whereas Anselm centered his atoning work in his death on the cross. [passive obedience] In this also Luther often centers his doctrine of the atonement, for the vicarious propitiatory death of our Lord was the culmination of his willing obedience to his Father's will. After all, according to Luther, there is only one atoning obedience of Christ, though it has two aspects, which after all are one; for us transgressors he kept the Divine law, which we had broken; for us transgressors he suffered and died to make satisfaction for our sins.[5]

---

3. Mueller, "Luther's Doctrine of the Atonement."
4. Luther, *Gospel Sermon, Good Friday* quoted in Kerr, *A Compend of Luther's Theology*, 54.
5. Mueller, "Luther's Doctrine of the Atonement."

Several factors informed Luther's views on the work of Christ:

1) The existential. He laid emphasis on the *pro me*, thus pointing beyond the redemptive facts to their meaning *for me*. It was this element that gave power to his preaching and teaching and came to be largely lost among his successors (see below). As Wallace so beautifully put it, "Luther *felt* the cross as vividly as he *saw* the cross."[6]

2) His nominalist training. His education was in Occamist philosophy, which emphasized the primacy of will over nature. This created a problem for him in seeking to find a gracious God. What was important was knowing God's attitude toward him, but God's inscrutable will was difficult to discern.

3) The *communicatio idiomatum* interpretation of Christology applied to soteriology. The communication of properties was Luther's way of explaining the way in which the God-man could be both human and divine. The human properties were communicated to the divine, and the divine properties were communicated to the human.[7]

This last point becomes the theological basis for what has been referred to as the "wonderful exchange." Luther expresses it clearly in his *Treatise on Christian Liberty*. Here he compares the relation between Christ and the church to a marriage bond. "Faith," he says, "unites the soul with Christ as a bride is united with her bridegroom." The point is that in this union what belongs to the bride becomes the groom's and what belongs to the groom becomes the bride's. Thus the righteousness (ethical) of the groom (Christ) is attributed to the bride (the church) and the sinfulness of the bride is attributed to the groom. In dramatic language he describes this wonderful exchange: ". . . He by the wedding–ring of faith shares in the sins, death and pains of hell which are His bride's, nay, makes them His own, and acts as if they were His own, and as if He Himself had sinned; He suffered, died and descended into hell that He might overcome them all."[8]

Despite his revolutionary discoveries and radical reorientation of soteriological theology, Luther remains solidly within the legal presuppositions of Western theology based on the concept of merit. He abandoned the possibility that human persons can earn sufficient merit to qualify for

---

6. Wallace, *The Atoning Death of Christ*, 77.

7. As we shall see below, Calvin did not accept this view as seriously as Luther.

8. Quoted in Wallace, *The Atoning Death of Christ*, 59.

acceptance with God but since merit remains, in his understanding, as the basis of acceptance, he shifts its locus to Christ. Thus the believer is saved on the basis of an alien righteousness, attributed to him or her from the righteousness of Christ. Justification by faith is thus vouchsafed but the question of sin is not dealt with. The believer is now *simul justus et peccator*, at the same time both justified and a sinner.

John Wesley reacted vigorously to this legal fiction insisting that God is not deceived in those whom He justifies. He does not account "them to be otherwise than they are. It does by no means imply, that God judges concerning us contrary to the real nature of things; that he esteems us better than we really are, or believes us righteous when we are unrighteous."[9] Yet he also resists the Catholic position that justification means "the being made actually just and righteous."

John Calvin

Few works of theology have had a greater influence on subsequent theological thought than Calvin's *Institutes of the Christian Religion*. It continues to be the benchmark for Reformed theology and even those who may disagree with Calvin's views find rich insights in his writing. It has with considerable justification been called the masterpiece of Protestant theology.[10]

For Calvin, the human situation is hopeless apart from the divine initiative. All that we had possessed, we had possessed by our divine communication.[11] This relation was lost in the fall resulting in an alienation from God, which brought us under the wrath of God, and deprived humanity of all free will in relation to God.

As seriously as Calvin takes the fall of man, he insists that it was not a fall out of the realm of God's love. He supports this position by a quote from St. Augustine:

> For it was not after we were reconciled to him by the blood of his Son that he began to love us, but he loved us before the foundation of the world, that with his only-begotten Son we too might be sons of God before we were anything at all. Our being reconciled by the death of Christ must not be understood as if the Son reconciled us, in order that the Father, then hating, might begin to love us, but

---

9. Sermon on "Justification by Faith," Wesley, *Works*, 5:53–64.

10. Quoted in Franks, *The Work of Christ*, from Albrecht Ritschl, 333.

11. John Calvin, *Institutes of the Christian Religion*, II.2.1. References to the *Institutes* will be inserted in the text by book, chapter and section, thus they may be checked in any translation or edition.

that we were reconciled to Him already loving, though at enmity with us because of sin. (II.16.4)

Nevertheless, men cannot honestly evaluate themselves

> without feeling that God is angry and at enmity with [them], and therefore anxiously longing for the means of regaining his favour (this cannot be without satisfaction), the certainty here required is of no ordinary description,—sinners, until freed from guilt, being always liable to the wrath and curse of God, who, as he is a just judge, cannot permit his law to be violated with impunity, but is armed for vengeance. (II.16.1)

This quotation incidentally demonstrates how Calvin assumes that God is amenable to law but in his own exposition, he recognizes that it raises the question of a contradiction, or apparent contradiction, between love and justice. "How can it be said," he asks, "that God, who prevents [precedes] us with his mercy, was our enemy until he was reconciled to us by Christ?" He attempts to solve the contradiction by appealing to his doctrine of accommodation. The scripture lays primary emphasis on guilt, wrath and justice for pedagogical purposes, that is, so that "we may the better understand how miserable and calamitous our condition is without Christ" (2.16.2). This ploy, however, does not remove the contradiction but only heightens it.

Oddly enough, Calvin affirms that this so-called pedagogical emphasis is true since God does in fact hate us because of our corrupt nature and "the depraved conduct following upon it . . . We are all offensive to God, guilty in his sight, and by nature the children of hell." Until this offensiveness is removed "by the expiation set forth in the death of Christ" so that "we, formerly impure and unclean, now appear in his sight just and holy" we have no hope of God being propitious towards us (2.16.3). Note the significance of the term "appear," which is to be taken in contrast to reality.

The manifestation of his love is in his gift of a mediator whose "work is to restore us to the divine favor, so as to make us, instead of sons of men, sons of God; instead of heirs of hell, heirs of a heavenly kingdom." The only one who could do this is the Son of God who became son of man so as to "receive what is ours" and "transfer to us what is his, making that which is his by nature to become ours by grace" (II.12.2). Here is Calvin's answer to Anselm's question, *Cur Deus Homo* as well as his statement of the wonderful exchange.

The reason for the incarnation is the fall. Unlike Eastern Orthodoxy, which taught that the incarnation would have occurred even if there had been no sin in order to facilitate mankind's growth in the likeness of God, Calvin vigorously rejects this "idle speculation." That position was taught by one of his contemporaries, Osiander, and Calvin strongly maligns him for this (2.12.4–7).

However Calvin, like Aquinas, rejects Anselm's doctrine of an absolute necessity of the incarnation. Although the redeemer must be "very God and very Man," he declares, "If the necessity be inquired into, it was not what is commonly termed simple or absolute, but flowed from the divine decree on which the salvation of man depended. What was best for us, our most merciful Father determined" (2.12.1). In a word, God simply willed it to be that way. It was not the result of either moral or metaphysical necessity.

How then is the enmity between God and man removed? We have already glimpsed a clue in the previously noted references. We must become "pure and clean, just and holy." Calvin's answer is that Christ accomplishes this through "the whole course of his obedience" (2.16.5). Thus, through his perfect obedience, Christ was completely acceptable to God in his own person. "Our acquittal is in this—that the guilt which made us liable to punishment was transferred to the head of the Son of God (Isa 53:12). We must specially remember this substitution in order that we may not be all our lives in trepidation and anxiety, as if the just vengeance, which the Son of God transferred to himself were still impending over us" (2.16.5).

Even though Calvin, like Luther, holds to a wonderful exchange, there emerges here an important qualification. Although Christ suffers in our stead and is punished in our place, it is only in his human nature that He does so. In affirming the reason for the incarnation, Calvin says:

> Our Lord came forth very man, adopted the person of Adam, and assumed his name, that he might in his stead obey the Father; that he might present our flesh as the price of satisfaction to the just judgment of God, and in the same flesh pay the penalty which we had incurred. Finally, since as God only he could not suffer, and as man only could not overcome death, he united the human nature with the divine, that he might subject the weakness of the one to death as an expiation of sin, and by the power of the other, maintaining a struggle with death, might gain us the victory. (2.12.3)

What we see here is Calvin's acceptance of the traditional understanding of God derived from Greek philosophy that God is passive, i.e. cannot suffer and therefore is not really involved in the redemptive process except as originating the incarnation which, as a result, is really then not taken with full seriousness. Even though he specifically rejects the heresy of Nestorianism (2.14.4) he clearly shows Nestorian tendencies here, which could be attributed to his rejection, with Zwingli, of a real *communicatio idiomatum* between the divine and human natures in the person of Christ. He would admit only a verbal *communicatio idiomatum*, referring to it as "a figure of speech" (II.14.1–2)[12] thus resulting in a distinction of natures that in turn becomes a distinction in the work of Christ, a division of labor as it were.

Calvin's idea of substitution is clearly seen in his view of sacrifice. His use of the Old Testament sacrificial system lays more emphasis on the victim than the priest although both are seen as substitutionary. Here he follows Augustine who says "in the Jewish ceremonies there was more a confession than an expiation of sins. For what more was done in sacrifice by those who substituted purifications instead of themselves, than to confess that they were conscious of deserving death" (II.7.17). The victim was their substitute to take the punishment that they deserved, and therefore the very act of sacrifice should teach men their own inability to sustain God's wrath, and their need for a representative. In fulfilling the priestly office of the Old Covenant, Christ fulfilled the whole of the sacrificial system by becoming that substitute for us, which was prefigured by the sacrificial victim.

All this depicts the atonement as objective in nature but Calvin, like Luther, insists that the *pro nobis* must be supplemented by a *pro me*. That is, for the work of Christ to be effective, we must appropriate it through faith. But faith is not a human possibility, it is exclusively the gift of the Holy Spirit. In his commentary on John 14:16, Calvin says: "The peculiar office of Christ was to appease the wrath of God by atoning for the sins of the world, to redeem men from death, to procure righteousness and life; the peculiar office of the Spirit is to make us partakers not only of Christ Himself, but of all His blessings."

Such a statement sets up a tension in Calvin between the universality of the atonement and the fact that not all believe in Him. Christ died for all men in obedience to the Father's will; faith is the gift of God, but only some men receive it. His answer is the doctrine of predestination and election. His own words are clear: "Let us remember, on the other hand, that while life is promised universally to all who believe in Christ, still faith is by no means common to all. For Christ is made known and held out to the sight of all, but the elect alone are those whose eyes God opens, that

---

12. Franks, *The Work of Christ*, 358.

they may seek Him by faith" (com. John 3:16). We are asked to pray that all men may be saved, for we do not know which men have been chosen to be saved; but we do know that God will save only those whom he has elected to salvation, and not the reprobate (com. John 17:9).

Though the provisions of the atonement may be inclusive, the results are exclusive because the effectual call is extended to only the elect and the end result is the same. In a word, Calvin's theology does not include the whole Christ for the whole world.

Protestant Orthodoxy

The development of atonement theology in the Protestant West reached its culmination (and lowest point) in the seventeenth century with Protestant Scholasticism (Orthodoxy). The existential nature of the work of Luther and Calvin was replaced by a rationalistic approach to theology that took its point of departure from the doctrine of particular predestination. One of the most influential figures here was Theodore Beza who assumed leadership of the training school at Geneva that had been founded and headed by Calvin himself.

This theology focused on those passages in Calvin that dealt with the penal aspect of the atonement and, as Ronald Wallace comments, "this particular aspect received an almost exclusive priority." Legal demands became paramount. God, as judge, is bound to act in accordance with so–called principles of absolute justice, which demand the retributive punishment of those who break the law. God accepted Christ as a substitute and punishes him instead of the sinner and God is satisfied.[13]

The heritage of Tertullian reached its full flower in this movement as the ideas of merit and satisfaction became the touchstones of theological soundness and the Western style courtroom served as the paradigm for understanding the divine-human relation.[14]

In a pivotal paragraph, Wallace captures the essence of the "orthodox" view of the work of Christ:

> It was not surprising, then, that they clarified the work done in the atonement by selecting the one aspect that could be most easily understood. The effect of giving the doctrine of predestination a dominant place led to the assertion that the atonement was limited in its scope—sometimes called the doctrine of a particular

---

13. Wallace, *The Atoning Death of Christ*, 83.

14. Albert Outler has a brief but helpful discussion of this fact in *Theology in the Wesleyan Spirit*, 51.

or limited atonement, in contrast to the doctrine of a universal atonement. Christ, it was asserted, died only for the elect. This was an assertion Calvin had never seriously discussed, but it now became important in reformed circles.[15]

Two comments need to be made here. The first sentence of this summary statement illuminates why this penal theory is so popular in folk theology and so difficult to dislodge even with those whose central theological commitments are inconsistent with it. It is easy to preach and simple to grasp, having tremendous emotional appeal if presented with the right analogies. Second, it is this development that results in what has been popularly referred to as the Calvinistic TULIP resulting in a tension between Calvin and "Calvinism."[16]

The rationalism and spiritual sterility that tended to accompany "orthodoxy" resulted in a number of reactions in the name of vital piety and also in alternate versions of the work of Christ. To some of these we turn in the next chapter.

---

15. Ibid., 84.

16. Total depravity, Unconditional election, Limited atonement, Irresistible grace and Perseverance of the saints.

5

Responses to "Orthodoxy"

Orthodoxy and heresy, are interesting concepts. When we look at their history it becomes rather clear that they are contextual terms. Orthodoxy refers to the validity of a teaching acknowledged, approved and defended by a given group. Heresy is what does not conform to this group's belief. The most general context in which the term might legitimately be used in a Christian sense is that of the undivided, or ecumenical, church of the first few centuries. It was out of this context that the so–called ecumenical creeds were formulated addressing the issues of the trinity and the person of Christ. These creeds, along with the Apostles' Creed are generally accepted among Christians as constituting the parameters of orthodoxy for the classical Christian faith. Quasi-Christian groups who reject these theological benchmarks are usually regarded as sects, or cults that propagate heresy.

Subsequently, the content of orthodoxy and heresy became a more restricted matter, depending on the context in which the terms were used. Often they have been connected with political power and authority. This, in brief, is the way in which the term "orthodoxy" came to be applied to the Protestant theology about the work of Christ against which we are proposing a protest.

Jaroslav Pelikan illustrates the contextual character of orthodoxy in an essay arguing that there is not a one-to-one relation between fundamentalism and orthodoxy. On each of the so-called fundamentals of the faith defended by the early twentieth century movement, he shows how there have been a variety of interpretations of each of the doctrines defended by fundamentalism and all within the pale of acceptable orthodoxy. He says: "Orthodoxy was not a straight line, but a circle drawn about a variety of permissible views, excluding other views."[1]

Is there a way of legitimating the concept of orthodoxy and/or heresy in the contemporary context? Probably not to everyone's satisfaction.

---

1. Pelikan, "Fundamentalism and/or Orthodoxy," 8.

However, one of the most promising suggestions of identifying both of these comes from the 19th century theologian, F. D. E. Schleiermacher whose *Christian Faith* is one of the classics in the history of Christian theological writing.

Schleiermacher argued that heresy was that which preserved the appearance of Christianity, but contradicted its essence. He wrote:

> If the distinctive essence of Christianity consists in the fact that in it all religious emotions are related to the redemption wrought by Jesus Christ, there will be two ways in which heresy can arise. That is to say: This fundamental formula will be retained in general . . . but either human nature will be so defined that a redemption in the strict case cannot be accomplished, or the Redeemer will be defined in such a way that he cannot accomplish redemption.[2]

A cursory look at the struggles in the early church about the relation between the divine and human natures of the person of Christ will demonstrate that this principle was at work in seeking to define the orthodox understanding. If Schleiermacher's insightful interpretation can be accepted, it becomes clear that the soteriological implications of any proposed explanation of the person and work of Christ may function as the touchstone of orthodoxy. With this in mind, what can we say about the so-called orthodox view of the atonement, namely, some form of the satisfaction theory? Its logical entailments result in heresy!

We have already noted certain deficiencies in this approach to which Wesleyan theologians have repeatedly called attention. It would be redundant to repeat these here. But there are also further problems. James S. Stewart, in a trenchant criticism of this orthodox position says: "Its greatest merit was the serious view it took of sin. Its greatest defect was its disastrous view of God. The adjective is not too strong." He quotes with approval the words of A. D. Lindsay: "When the atonement is presented in that form, it seems as though the redeeming love of Christ could save men, but not God, as though God was the one person who was beyond redemption." Very pointedly Stewart remarks, "It cannot be too firmly emphasized that the whole idea of propitiating God is radically unscriptural."[3]

In this light, it is no wonder that there early appeared responses to the orthodox position offering alternate understandings of the work of Christ. We now survey a few of the more important ones:

---

2. Quoted in McGrath, *Christian Theology*, 147.
3. Stewart, *A Man in Christ*, 217.

Socinianism

Socinianism is the teaching of Faustus Socinus (d. 1604) who was generally recognized as a heretic because of his anti–trinitarian teaching and other deviations from traditional views. However, we must avoid an *ad hominem* here by not rejecting what Socinus says about the work of Christ because he held these heretical views on other matters. In fact, R. S. Franks commented that "Socinus not infrequently gives the true interpretation [of scripture] where the previous exegesis was wrong." In expounding the view of Socinus about the work of Christ, Franks notes that "Socinianism is to be understood as the product of a union between the humanism of Erasmus and the logical criticism of the school of Duns Scotus, effected in a mind liberated by the Reformation from the authority of the Church, but unsubjugated by Luther's new religious principle of justification by faith."[4]

This seems to necessitate a brief look at the views of Duns Scotus (d. 1308). With Scotus the contrast between the intellectualists and the voluntarists reached its most critical stage. Based on his radical empirical epistemology, Duns held that all theological knowledge is revealed and arbitrary, not accessible by natural reason. This is because all theological truth is a revelation of God's otherwise inscrutable will. *Will* is the operative word here. This meant that transcendent doctrines were not susceptible to rational proof other than by reference to the arbitrary sovereign will of God, which has decreed that certain things must be.[5]

Duns agrees with main stream medieval soteriology by affirming that God has ordained that human salvation must take place by way of merit simply because God has willed it to be so. In similar fashion, he defines merit in terms of will. Merit has value only when it is willed to be so and God accepts it as merit only because He wills to do so. The work of Christ provides merit because He wills it to be so but because it is the work of his human nature (not the divine nature; not even in conjunction with the divine as Anselm) his merit is finite and therefore logically is meritorious for only those whom God wills it to be, thus the logical basis for predestination.

In the light of this, we can see the import of Socinus' insistence that if the idea of satisfaction was simply the manifestation of God's will, there is no reason why He could not will to forgive sin without satisfaction. Among those who were voluntarists, there was no real basis for refutation of his conclusion. The only other option was to appeal to God's essential

---

4. Franks, *The Work of Christ*, 362.
5. Ibid., 236.

nature but epistemological access to this source of information was becoming increasingly problematic.

Unfortunately Socinus followed the teaching that "Christ suffered as a man, for God is impassible. Hence His sufferings cannot possess infinite value."[6] We have previously seen how the idea of the impassible nature of God has precluded the possibility of seeing how God Himself can be involved in the redemptive process.

This is such an important consideration that it is worth emphasizing here that the idea of the impassibility of God is an alien import from Greek philosophy that became deeply embedded in the Christian theological tradition. Alister McGrath refers to this idea as a classic example of how Christianity often unconsciously absorbs ideas and values from its cultural backdrop. His conclusion is significant for our purposes: "It points to the fact that there is a provisional or conditional element to Christian theology, which is not necessitated by or implied in its foundational resources. In other words, certain ideas which have often been regarded as Christian ideas often turn out to be ideas imported from a secular context."[7] Later on we shall see how the abandonment of this traditional (alien) concept will open the door to a sounder theological understanding of the atonement.

It should be seen from this discussion that Socinus' views on the atonement are faulty because of his doctrine of God, informed by medieval scholasticism rather than by the incarnation, taken as definitive of the divine nature and involving a genuine union of the divine and human natures.

It should also be observed here that Wesleyan theology insists that God's nature, not his will, is primary and thus practically takes sides with the intellectualists even though Wesley himself rejects this psychologizing analysis of God.[8] This move makes our understanding of the divine nature critical to a proper interpretation of the atonement. The crucial question concerns the source of this understanding. Is it scripture or tradition?

Arminianism

Within the bounds of more traditional Christian theology, the most significant response to Calvinism came from a movement known as Arminianism, stemming from the controversies surrounding the Dutch pastor and theology professor, James Arminius (1560–1609). However,

---

6. Ibid., 370.
7. McGrath, *Christian Theology*, 121.
8. See Dunning, *Grace, Faith and Holiness*, 196.

discussions of Arminianism relating to atonement theology do not usually refer to Arminius himself but move directly to the teachings of his followers, particularly the work of Hugo Grotius whose Governmental theory of the atonement is viewed as the definitive interpretation of the Arminian position. I think it is most important to be aware of Arminius' own views first since many of his followers moved in a liberalizing direction.

When Arminius was called to Amsterdam to become pastor of the Dutch Reformed Church after a brilliant career as a student, he found himself in a tension–filled situation that had developed over a long period of time. The Reformation in Holland was practically an indigenous affair that involved both religion and politics. It came about after many struggles and not a little bloodshed due to the dominance of the Roman Catholic Church.[9]

According to Carl Bangs, the term "Reformed" in the Christianity of the Low Countries "carries the special connotation of Zwinglian and Calvinist sympathy vis-à-vis the Lutherans, and this meaning applies to the Amsterdam Reformers, but with local qualifications."[10] In a word, the Dutch Reformation was tolerant and best described as a mild Calvinism quite different from the teachings of Theodore Beza referred to above. Bangs refers to some of the persons involved as Arminians before Arminius.

By the time of Arminius' entrance into the pastoral ministry, ministers who were staunch, hyper-Calvinists had become part of the Church in Holland and there was conflict between them and the moderate Calvinists.

By 1591, controversy began to surround Arminius over issues that Arminius describes in a letter to his old friend and teacher at the University of Basil, Grynaeus, who did not hold with Beza: "There is a lot of controversy among us about predestination, original sin, and free will." He includes in the letter the statement, "Our opponents, who are numerous here, deny [original sin] altogether." This reflects the fact that declaring them Socinians, or liberals has falsely maligned Arminius and his followers. They did not affirm free will but free grace.

There have been some interesting stories about Arminius' conversion to the position associated with his name, but Bangs demonstrates

---

9. In his definitive treatment of Arminius, Carl Bangs traces in careful detail the developments that resulted in the Dutch Reformed Church of Arminius' day. The material included in the text here draws upon Bangs' work but with the attempt to avoid the highly technical, and necessary, analysis in his book. Bangs should have full credit for the interpretations found herein, and not credited with any misinterpretation.

10. Ibid., 95.

rather conclusively that "Arminius was not in agreement with Beza's doctrine of predestination when he undertook his ministry at Amsterdam; indeed he probably never had agreed with it,"[11] even though he had studied under Beza.

The disagreements erupted into controversy out of Arminius' preaching on Romans 7 and seemed to reach their peak when he got to Romans 9. The issues were predestination and election. Arminius did not deny the doctrines of election and predestination but interpreted them as referring to "classes" rather than individuals. That is, God has predestined to salvation all those who believe in Christ.

One of the most illuminating aspects of this controversy was the continued, always postponed, plan to convene a national synod to settle the controversy. Arminius, along with some of his followers, were involved in a committee who were to formulate the ground rules for the synod when it did finally convene. One of the major issues concerned whether or not the disputants could appeal to scripture to support their arguments. Arminius and his people insisted that scripture should be used as authority but they were outvoted and the rule was established that the creeds (Belgic Confession and Heidelberg Catechism) were to be the final court of appeal.

Bang's trenchant words recount the sad aftermath: "There was a national synod, nine years after [Arminius'] death, the Synod of Dort of 1618–19, and so far was it from the vision of Arminius that the Arminians themselves were never even seated as delegates, but were only summoned as culprits to appear before it for condemnation."

It is obvious that little seems to be said in these controversies about the atonement but the *orthodox* understanding with its implications lies behind the whole controversy. It remained for Hugo Grotius (1583–1645), a law student at Leiden where Arminius was professor, to develop what has been described as an Arminian interpretation of the atonement, known as the Governmental Theory.

The Governmental Theory of Hugo Grotius.

Grotius' theory has influenced Arminian theologians to relatively recent times including many important Methodist theologians such as John Miley. Grotius developed his own views in the context of a refutation of Socinianism. The crux of his position is a distinction between the nature of God as Judge and his nature as a *Rector*, or Supreme Governor.

---

11. Ibid., 141.

Consequently, his view has been called the *rectoral* theory. A Judge operates *under* the law and therefore cannot free the guilty from punishment even by transferring it to another because he is the servant of the law. This right properly belongs only to the Supreme Governor. This is similar to the distinction Aquinas had made.

This would seem to be saying the same thing as Socinus, i.e. giving God (the supreme authority) the right to merely forgive, or to relax the law. Grotius rejects this conclusion however and seeks to "plow a middle furrow" between Socinus and orthodoxy. As Franks simply puts it: "The Divine act is therefore not the execution of the law; for then no sinner would escape eternal death. Nor yet is it the abrogation of the law; for an abrogated law has lost its obligation, yet unbelievers remain subject to the law."[12]

In this context, Grotius seeks to retain the substitutionary aspect of Christ's atonement but with two qualifications. It consists in suffering rather than punishment and it is conditional rather than absolute in nature. If sin is to be punished, it is not punished in Christ since the demerit of sin cannot be attributed to him. That is, he cannot be considered really guilty of the sin of someone else. Thus logically the law in its penalty is relaxed in every instance of non–execution upon the actual sinner.

It is incumbent upon the ruler, however, to maintain moral order for the good of the realm and, argues Grotius, God does this by Christ suffering the penalty of sin as an example of the consequences of sin to be suffered by those who continue therein. It seems, therefore, that the cross is a deterrent, thus a kind of moral influence theory in reverse. This is clearly seen in H. Orton Wiley's characterization of Grotius' view: "The death of Christ and His sufferings became, therefore, not an exhibition of love to draw men to God, as in the moral influence theories, but a deterrent to sin through an exhibition of its punishment."[13]

What we are seeing here is an attempt to find a way out of the implications of the satisfaction theory of the atonement that nonetheless remains solidly within the legal mentality that has informed the Western mind from the second century on. Grotius' tortured arguments seeking to modify this way of theologizing demonstrates the complexities of seeking to function in an alien context.

As R. Larry Shelton has shown, the followers of John Wesley have generally developed some form of the governmental theory, primarily,

---

12. Ibid., 394.

13. Wiley, *Christian Theology*, 2:252. Cf. Maddox's same evaluation, *Responsible Grace*, 108.

it seems, to avoid the logical implications of the penal substitutionary theory. But in the attempt to avoid a limited atonement and unconditional election on the one hand they have run the risk of universalism on the other.[14]

The major problem with this succession of Wesleyans, Shelton argues, is their effort to avoid the implications of Christ suffering the penalty for sin while at the same time maintaining that his sufferings were a substitute for penalty. He points out the dilemma of thus seeking to hold to two contradictory positions:

> It seems obvious that if [these] governmentalists see Christ's sacrifice as only a substitute for penalty, they cannot consistently describe His work as penal in any clear way. It appears that while the governmental theory rejects the penal substitution and unconditional election of Calvinism, it has not totally separated itself from the liabilities of a penal understanding of the atonement.[15]

It is the legal presupposition that needs to be called into question and the next response to "orthodoxy" we want to look at goes a long way toward doing just that.

John McLeod Campbell (1800–1872)

John McLeod Campbell's work on the atonement has been evaluated by some as one of the classics of all time on the subject.[16] Of considerable significance is the fact that this work grew out of Campbell's pastoral experience as an effort to find a way to address the practical problems of his parishioners. The story is filled with pathos and human interest.

Campbell was educated at Glasgow University and Divinity Hall and in 1825 was appointed pastor to the Parish of Rhu (Row) where he faithfully served for 5 years. He soon discovered among his parishioners an absence of the joy and sense of assurance he believed the New Testament taught to be the privilege of believers in Jesus Christ.

As he explored the reason for this, "the more he became convinced it was due to a 'legal strain' in their thinking that led to a want of true

---

14. It was apparently for this reason that Richard S. Taylor professedly abandoned a lifelong defense of the governmental theory for a penal satisfaction interpretation but attempted to avoid its implications by pronouncement rather than rationale. *God's Integrity and the Cross*, ix.

15. Shelton, "A Covenantal Concept of Atonement," 104.

16. James Torrance, Introduction to Campbell, *The Nature of the Atonement*, 2.

religion in the land."[17] The theology that informed their religious life was Federal Calvinism. According to this teaching,

> God had made a Covenant, or contract, with Christ whereby he would be gracious toward certain ones on the conditions that Christ die for their sins. But how could one know whether he was one of the elect? In order to answer this question, the Practical Syllogism was developed: Major premiss [sic]: The truly penitent person is one of God's elect. Minor Premiss [sic]: (based on self–examination) I have repented. Conclusion: Therefore I am (probably) one of the elect. But such a conviction, warned the Westminster Confession, might only be reached after a lifetime of doubt and struggle.[18]

Searching the New Testament, Campbell found a different picture of God, a God of grace and love who freely offered forgiveness that is not conditioned by considerations of worth and merit. He began preaching this message with transforming results in his church. The congregation flourished, the joy was abundant and his people became a vibrant group of followers of Christ. As visitors to this rural parish came to escape the city (Edinburgh) they carried back reports of the preaching and its results. The end result was that various ecclesiastical groups in the Church of Scotland called Campbell on the carpet until finally he was tried before the General Assembly in May, 1831 and was deposed from the ministry.

Eloquent appeals were made on his behalf, including one heart wrenching one from his father who was also a minister, but to no avail. Those who have read the proceedings report that it was a travesty. One of the more interesting aspects, which gives us a feeling of *déjà vu* was that Campbell was forbidden to appeal to scripture in his own defense. The argument was that he had been ordained on the basis of subscribing to the creed and he must now be judged by faithfulness to it (remember the Arminian controversy!).

The charges against him said:

> . . . *the doctrine of universal atonement* and pardon through the death of Christ, as also the doctrine that *assurance is of the essence of faith* and necessary for salvation are contrary to the Holy Scripture and to the Confession of Faith approven [sic] by the General Assemblies of the Church of Scotland, and ratified by law in the year sixteen hundred and ninety: and were moreover condemned

17. Ibid.
18. Thimell, "Christ in Our Place," 182–83.

by the fifth act of the General Assembly held in seventeen hundred and twenty, as being directly opposed to the Word of God, and to the Confession of Faith and Catechisms of the Church of Scotland . . . .[19] (*Proceedings* I.1)

In 1833 some interested friends secured him a chapel in Blackfriers Street, Glasgow. Here he served for about 25 years, except for a few intervals due to poor health.

When Campbell's treatise on the atonement was finally published (with some trepidation by the publishers because of his difficult writing style) it took some time to be recognized. His father is reported to have remarked: "Man, you have a queer way of putting things." Tuttle accurately describes his style which is exceedingly difficult to follow: "The sentences are long and involved, with qualifying words and clauses placed in an unusual order whereby the reader may easily miss the thread of a thought, though a slight pause for examination lays bare a consistently logical argument."[20]

Campbell's logical acumen recognized that the previous statements of the work of Christ had been developed by beginning with certain presuppositions, presuppositions that he felt needed critical examination. He recognized that beginning with faulty assumptions resulted in faulty conclusions. There was no problem with the deductive process, but with the presuppositions. For example, one of those whose views he carefully examined (and rejected) was that of John Owen, whose spirituality and mental powers he admired. He admitted the unassailable logic of Owen's system by which he would have felt himself bound if only he could accept Owen's presuppositions. There was the rub. On this same logical basis, he not only rejected the older Calvinism [orthodoxy] but also what he called the modified Calvinism as taught by Grotius (specifically he referred to other teachers of the governmental theory)

Campbell believed that the first step in atonement discussion should be a study of the biblical account of Christ's work. If one yields oneself to the mind of Christ as revealed through the New Testament then certain fundamental ideas commend themselves to conscience as the proper foundations upon which to begin constructing a statement on the nature of the atonement. Hence he set out to self-consciously develop *The Nature of the Atonement* on presuppositions derived from scripture.

---

19. Quoted by Torrance, "Introduction," 2.

20. Tuttle, *So Rich a Soil*, 99. My own reading of Campbell has verified the validity of this judgment.

In a word, he accepted the general principle that the atonement should be seen by its own light. Tuttle suggests four presuppositions derived from this principle (verified by my own reading of Campbell):

1) The Atonement Originates in the Love of God.

While the love of God has never been entirely lost to view in any statement of the atonement claiming to be Christian, in both forms of Calvinism to which Campbell was exposed, the requirements of justice assumed the primary importance. This meant that the atonement must precede forgiveness. "But," says Campbell, "the scriptures do not speak of such an atonement; for they do not represent the atonement of Christ as the cause, but, just the contrary—they represent the love of God as the cause, and the atonement as the effect." Therefore it is important to remember that forgiveness, as the form in which love is manifested, precedes the atonement, and that any statement on the atonement should always have this clearly in view. It is against a loving Father that we have sinned; and to such we are reconciled. This is the pivotal point of Campbell's whole discussion of the atonement. If reconciling love and justice requires giving primacy to one or the other, then love must be first. He is thoroughly Wesleyan at this point.

This does not invalidate the necessity for ethical righteousness since the God of love both demands and yearns for a filial righteousness. We can only be received when coming to the parent God as sons and daughters rightly relating ourselves to God and to one another—not otherwise. Campbell thus contends that it is utterly false to associate moral weakness with the nature of divine love, which includes righteousness. Though founding atonement on the fatherliness of God was novel at the time, he believed that he was only developing a doctrine implicit in the New Testament.

2) The Atonement Contemplates God's Prospective Purpose that Humanity Shall be Sons and Daughters.

Here is one of Campbell's most significant insights. While every view of the atonement takes account of both the "retrospective" and the "prospective" aspects (Campbell's terms), Campbell felt that they had not been treated as organic aspects of the atonement. Reformation theology had generally treated the prospective as almost incidental whereas for Campbell, it was clearly the most important. So it becomes characteristic of Campbell's writing that the prospective purposes of the atonement are always brought into clear view as determinative of its nature. This is likewise true of Wesley, although using different concepts and terminology.

Here lies one of Campbell's major objections to founding a view of atonement on the concept of justice—whether distributive or rectoral. Both systems visualize what he calls purely legal atonements, that is, atonements, the whole character of which is determined by our relation to divine law. The real problem of atonement, however, is not merely to discover a way in which we may stand reconciled to God as a lawgiver. The question contemplated in scripture and to which the Gospel is an answer is not how we can be pardoned and receive mercy, but how it could come to pass that the estranged can be reconciled. God's intention is, as St. Paul declared, "to redeem those who were under the law, so that we might receive adoption as sons"(Gal 4:5).[21]

Campbell therefore could not rest in any conception of the atonement that involved, as he says, "the substitution of a legal standing for a filial standing as the gift of God to men in Christ."

The atonement is thus revealed retrospectively as God's way of putting right the past, and prospectively as introducing us to a life marked by a filial relation to God eternally. Both are celebrated by believers, both must be included in their thought concerning the nature of the atonement.

3) The Atonement Presupposes the Incarnation of God in the Humanity of Jesus the Christ.

This is the issue of the relation of the incarnation to the atonement. Which has priority? Western orthodoxy has tended to treat the incarnation as necessary only in relation to the death of Christ (notably Anselm). While Campbell never removes himself from the Western tradition (to adopt the Eastern emphasis on the incarnation) he does take the incarnation with utmost seriousness. He insists that the fact of sin and the necessity for atonement must be seen in the light of the incarnation. This implies that in Christ, God as God *is* confronts us with pardon, and grace to engage in God's way. When therefore it is said that Christ represents God to us it can only be in the sense that in and through Christ God is present to us as God really is (note difference from Calvin). This further means that he emphasizes the importance of the life as well as of the death of Jesus. The death is the necessary outcome of that life in a sinful world. This means that whatever view is taken of the atoning death of Christ, it must be confirmed by an examination of the outward events of his life among people.

4) The Atonement is Mediated by Christ as Representative of a New Humanity.

---

21. Ibid., 82.

This addresses the manner of the incarnation. If Christ is but an individual, atomistically considered, he can be a moral example or a substitute for all individuals with the exchange of guilt and righteousness by imputation resulting in a legal fiction. But Campbell had given up on this. Perhaps Christ is humanity in a collective or corporate sense. Campbell is rather obscure and had difficulty articulating clearly what he thought on this matter. However, the thought of Christ as our representative commended itself to Campbell as taking into account the fact that we, because of Christ's identification with us, are included in Christ's work.

James B. Torrance, Campbell's champion in contemporary theology, has attempted to develop this more clearly and fully in relation to worship in an essay entitled "The Vicarious Humanity of Christ" in a volume on *The Incarnation* edited by T. F. Torrance.[22]

Obviously, Campbell made significant steps forward by identifying the Achilles' heel of the various satisfaction theories of the atonement, directing our attention to the nature of God as defined by the incarnation, and highlighting the nature of the divine-human relation as personal rather than legal or impersonal. However, in spite of all these tremendous insights he still remained somewhat within the limitations of the Western tradition so that his most unique contribution (vicarious repentance, which his supporters have struggled manfully to defend) still is susceptible to the criticism of D. C. Mackintosh: ". . . his own mind was still somewhat confused, as he groped his pioneering way toward that thoroughly rational and ethical view of reconciliation with God to which he perhaps never quite attained: because he shared the 'traditional concept of propitiation sacrifice,'" resulting in "the self–contradictory notion of a God already propitious enough to provide the propitiatory offering which is to propitiate Himself."[23]

One of Campbell's most important contributions was his emphasis on both the retrospective and the prospective aspects of the atonement. He recognized that satisfaction theories primarily focused on the former but had no essential place for the latter and it was this that was the fundamental New Testament emphasis on the work of Christ: to accomplish God's redemptive intention for the human race, in a word, sanctification as the renewal of persons in the image of God.

22. Torrance, ed., *The Incarnation*.

23. Mackintosh, "Two Important Books of Theology," 460–61. Unfortunately, Macintosh's critique is made from a perspective that attributes this self-contradictory idea to St. Paul. More recent biblical scholarship has exposed the fallacy of attributing this to Paul (see discussion in chapter 8).

6

Atonement: Objective or Subjective

DISCUSSIONS ABOUT the atonement have oscillated between objective and subjective interpretations of it. Those who insist on an objective atonement see it as something done by Christ quite apart from our knowledge of it and its effect upon us.[1] The subjective view sees it as a reconciling of us to God through a persuasion in our hearts that God accepts us because of his eternal love. Anselm and Calvin are classic proponents of the objective interpretation while exemplarist views epitomize the subjective. Perhaps it is largely a matter of emphasis since few would totally exclude one or the other but it does constitute a watershed issue.

While the language of objective/subjective is not prominent (if present at all) in the Eastern fathers, the issue was still present. In interpreting the incarnation as the atonement, the union of the divine and human could be seen as more or less automatically "divinizing" human nature by virtue of the theanthropic union of the two natures. Certain critics have accused the realistic theory of redemption found in the patristic fathers as having just this implication.

The tension between these two understandings became most prominent in the West. Some form of the transactional theory seemed to be the only possibility of an objective interpretation of the work of Christ. But the implications drove those at whom we looked in the last chapter (and many others as well) toward the subjective view. An objective theory viewed in transactional terms seemed logically to entail a theory of particular election and predestination. Those who subscribe to this approach are thus apparently compelled by their presuppositions to characterize any other explanation as a moral influence theory.

In our discussion of John McLeod Campbell, we noted that his critique of John Owen's doctrine pointed out how Owen's presuppositions led logically to certain conclusions that Campbell found to be antithetical

---

1. Although perhaps a bit too simple, Richard S. Taylor gives a clear definition: "By 'objective' is meant the nature of the Atonement as a transaction between the Father and the Son" (*God's Integrity and the Cross*, 20).

to the New Testament. He concluded that it was the presuppositions that needed to be examined critically. A brief look at Owen's argument may be instructive.

Owen's arguments against the Arminian doctrine of universal redemption demonstrate the rationale just described. It is very similar to Anselm's reasoning. On the premise that what God intended by the work of Christ must be accomplished, he reaches the conclusion that the Arminian position implied that Christ's work has in reality done nothing at all, since it has actually and effectively saved no one. Since Owen taught that both Christ's death and his heavenly intercession are included in his atoning work, he concludes that he "neither offered Himself nor interceded for any but the elect."[2]

In a word, the atonement strictly interpreted in an objective sense seems to lead unavoidably to the Reformed position of election and predestination *if* it is seen only as a transaction occurring between the Son and the Father.

A number of factors emerged in the modern period that led to a widespread reaction against orthodoxy and a move toward a more subjective view of the atonement. One of the factors was the turn toward the subject in the philosophy of the eighteenth century. René Descartes' search for certainty, which he found via his famous *cogito ergo sum*, implied the belief that the only sure knowledge was to be found in the contents of the mind. The analyses of the capability of the human mind by David Hume and Immanuel Kant further called into question the possibility of purely objective knowledge. Robert H. King, in exploring the paradigm shifts that took place during this pivotal period of history noted: "After Kant it would be difficult to make any kind of knowledge claim without taking into account the knowing subject. While not perceived as the immediate threat that science represented, this development too constituted a challenge to the theological tradition, since it brought into question the objectivity of many of its claims."[3]

While these developments were primarily related to epistemological matters, they fostered a mood that impacted thinking about the work of Christ. They pressed theologians who sought to actualize the Christian faith in the contemporary situation to look for new ways of establishing their truth claims.

One of the most important of these was F. D. E. Schleiermacher. As Schleiermacher perceived the situation, no longer could Christian claims

---

2. Franks, *The Work of Christ*, 463.
3. King, "Introduction: The Task of Theology," 12.

be based on knowledge as if it were science, or on ethics (as Kant had proposed). Therefore he argued that religion was a unique phenomenon characterized by a particular kind of feeling. Specifically it was the *feeling of absolute dependence* or positively stated, *God-consciousness*.[4]

The perfect embodiment of God-consciousness is found only in Jesus of Nazareth whereby he becomes the redeemer by virtue of stimulating a God-consciousness in us. In Schleiermacher's words, "The Redeemer assumes believers into the power of his God-consciousness, and this is His redemptive activity."[5] Here we have a thoroughly subjective view that is a sophisticated version of the moral influence theory. However Schleiermacher moves beyond the typical exemplarist views by arguing that Jesus is more than a pattern or example for us, he is the archetype, i.e., the type or pattern that has the power of reproducing itself in others. However, H. D. McDonald is doubtless correct when he says: "Here is a subjective view of the work of Christ that fails altogether to accord to his death any objective significance for man's salvation."[6]

It was Schleiermacher's emphasis on experience that made him the father of theological liberalism. The centrality of experience in liberal thought resulted in the minimizing of the historical or objective aspect of the work of Christ but it did highlight the importance of experience. This concern for what we would call today the existential aspect of the atonement is well expressed in the work of R. C. Moberly who attempted to maintain both the objective and the subjective interpretations but clearly rejected the transactional understanding that was characteristic of orthodoxy.

Moberly stated that "one primary difficulty to our thought is the conviction . . . that whatever happened on Calvary, did not happen to us." The following quotation captures his perspective succinctly:

> Whether we go to more ancient or to more modern, forms of current explanation,—whether the paying of a ransom, or the canceling of a debt, or the substitution of a victim, is our leading metaphor,—there is one thing which seems, at first sight, to belong alike to all views which start from the great historical event, and find their explanation within that: namely that, characterize it how they may, they seem to make atonement a transaction, historical,

---

4. For a good analysis of both Kant and Schleiermacher vis-à-vis the atonement, see Gunton, *The Actuality of the Atonement*, 3–16.

5. Schleiermacher, *The Christian Faith*, 431.

6. McDonald, *The Atonement of the Death of Christ*, 214. McDonald throughout is implicitly defending the penal theory.

> final, consummated long ago:—a transaction . . . far anterior to, and wholly outside of, the reality of ourselves.[7]

H. D. McDonald's evaluation of Moberly calls attention to the close affinities of his views with McLeod Campbell and his critique points out certain weaknesses that we will need to keep in mind as we move toward a constructive statement.

> It is a merit in the judgment of many that Moberly avoids any transactional idea of atonement and that he seeks to bring it into the sphere of personal and spiritual realities. On the other hand, Moberly does not secure his position of how Christ does, or can, repent of sins he did not himself commit . . . Nor yet, as in the case of Campbell, does his theory provide sufficient reason for Christ's death; for if the atonement is to be found in Christ's penitence, it is not easy to see why Christ must die. Nor yet is it clear how penitence as such could so affect God that he must needs suffer for it.[8]

Another development emerged during this general period among English theologians known as deists, who defended the rational nature of Christianity. In general it could be said that they rejected the "orthodox" view because of its interpretation of the nature of God. If God is essentially merciful, there is no need of an atonement that functions to satisfy or propitiate the divine nature. But the more significant point here is the beginnings of a most influential idea that pitted Jesus against Paul.[9]

Those who made the distinction between the teachings of Jesus and (primarily) the teaching of the Pauline Epistles insisted that the final authority here lies with the Gospels. The occasional nature of the epistles results in the accommodation of the gospel to specific situations but the teaching of Jesus about the readiness of God to forgive is in antithesis to what was understood to be the ideas found in Paul who had "perverted" the simple message of the Messiah.

There were still theologians in this period, however, who argued for the orthodox position. William Butler in his famous *Analogy of Religion* sought to demonstrate the consistency of the doctrine of the mediation of Christ in terms of *natural religion* by drawing an analogy between the idea

---

7. *Atonement and Personality*, 137–38. Moberly's work appeared later than that of R. W. Dale (see below) and in part was a critical response to it.

8. McDonald, *The Atonement of the Death of Christ*, 271. While McDonald is seeking to defend the viability of the penal theory, his criticisms may be answered in another way as we shall see further on.

9. This development seems to have appeared first with John Locke.

of divine punishment for sin and the consequences of sin in the natural order along with the necessity for a mediation to avoid these consequences.

Butler's argument was based on an assumption of Enlightenment science that the universe was governed by a rational system of laws guaranteed by an all-wise and benevolent Creator. These laws, discoverable by science, was held to be paralleled by laws in the spiritual realm that common sense could identify. This assumption informed Protestant evangelicalism in America throughout the nineteenth century, reinforced by the prevailing philosophy of Scottish Realism. This philosophy's decline in the general philosophical scene partially explains the rise of fundamentalism as a reactionary movement to modern science and secularization.[10]

As we have earlier noted, during the period dominated by theological liberalism, the prevailing tendency was toward the moral influence or subjective understanding and away from the objective, accompanied by an emphasis on the importance of the ethical life. This was doubtless an aspect of the optimism that was prevalent during this time. Horace Bushnell was one of the influential voices expressing this mood. Bushnell insisted that there are objective elements in the atonement. Christ's death, he declared, affects God, and expresses God. The following paragraph anticipates later developments in the doctrine of God regarding the question of his passibility that opens the door to a full divine participation in the atonement:

> Whatever we may say or hold or believe concerning the vicarious sacrifice of Christ, we are to affirm in the same manner of God. The whole Deity is in it, in it from eternity . . . There is a cross in God before the wood is seen on the hill . . . It is as if there were a cross unseen, standing on its undiscovered hill, far back in the ages.[11]

But there were still significant voices defending the orthodox view. One of the most celebrated of these defenses was the lectures of R. W. Dale who is described by McDonald as "no more profound an advocate of the penal doctrine of the atonement,"[12] and Franks says his "powerful book may be said to be perhaps the most forcible restatement in English of the orthodox theory of the atonement."[13]

However, Dale's work reflects some significant modifications of the traditional formulations, modifications that perhaps herald certain changes

---

10. Marsden, *Fundamentalism and American Culture*.

11. Quoted in McGrath, *Christian Theology*, 394. The view of the cross here is virtually reproduced by Baillie, *God was in Christ*, 192–94.

12. McDonald, *The Atonement*, 242.

13. Franks, *The Work of Christ*, 688; Dale, *The Atonement*.

in the general defense of the orthodox doctrine. Two related ideas inform the entirety of his Congregational Union lectures, delivered in 1875. First, the term "atonement" is understood to mean that God is, through the death of Christ, enabled to receive mankind into relation to himself. This presupposes that the term cannot be legitimately used of a merely moral influence theory. The second idea, based on this assumption is that the New Testament speaks with one voice in emphasizing the relation between the death of Christ and the remission of sins. Much of the lectures were given over to surveying the New Testament, including the Gospels, to demonstrate this point. It is this fact, rather than an articulated theory that demonstrates, according to Dale, the validity of the atonement understood in terms of the first presupposition.

One of Dale's concerns is to seek to prove that there is no diastasis between the teaching of Jesus and Pauline theology as had been suggested by liberal interpreters.[14] He does this by seeking to demonstrate that the whole of Jesus' ministry is focused toward his death, which is therefore more definitive for the remission of sins than his teachings.[15]

However, he does seek to give due regard to the subjective aspect of the work of Christ and thus maintains a kind of balance between the objective and subjective. In fact, in the extensive preface to the seventh edition,[16] he replies to a critic who had accused him of espousing the moral theory because of his heavy emphasis on the love of God as the originating cause of the atonement.

It is important to note that Dale's constructive statement makes much of the death of Christ fulfilling the "eternal law of righteousness," thus continuing the legal context (although significantly modified) that we have seen to inform most Western theologizing. But in spite of the glowing rec-

---

14. In lecture IV he says, "The tendency to discriminate between apostolic teaching and the teaching of the Lord Jesus Christ is, I believe, very general," 158. In lectures given in 1908, P. T. Forsyth addresses this issue with considerable energy: "In regard to Christ's cross, and within the New Testament, we are today face to face with a new situation. We are called upon, sometimes in the tones of a religious war, to set Jesus against Paul and to choose between the historic and the biblical Christ. We are bidden to release Jesus from Paul's arrest, to raise Him from that tomb in which He was buried by the apostle of the resurrection, and to loose Him and let Him go. The issue comes to a crisis in the interpretation of the death of Christ . . . To regard it as having anything to do with God's judgment on man's sin, or as being the ground of forgiveness, is a piece of grim Judaism or gloomy Paulinism" (*The Cruciality of the Cross*, 11).

15. He says, "Far more of God was revealed in what He was, in what He did, and in what He suffered, than in what He taught" (*The Atonement*, 98).

16. That Dale's lectures went through at least 24 editions testifies to its influence and popularity.

ommendation of Dale's work as a defense of the penal theory, he actually draws the stinger from this view as classically understood. In his restatement of his conception of the atonement, he affirms that the Lord suffered the penal consequences of sin but explicitly denies that there was any imputation of sin to Him, which would be a legal fiction. "But in a very real and deep sense, He made the consequences of our sin His own."[17]

A careful analysis of the lectures substantiates the validity of Franks' judgment that since there is "no talk of an equivalence in substituted punishment, . . . what we find is in essence the Grotian idea of a penal example."[18] Furthermore, one could also argue that Dale's explanation more accurately reflects a representative theory of the work of Christ based in part on his language but more upon his emphasis on the incarnation as Christ's full identification with mankind embodying the divinely intentioned relation of humanity to God. The consequence of this he explains thus: "The Death of Christ is the objective ground on which the sins of men are remitted, because it rendered possible the retention or the recovery of our original and ideal relation to God through Christ which sin had dissolved, and the loss of which was the supreme penalty of transgression."

Dale makes one further significant advance in the discussion. In earlier attempts of orthodoxy to explain the atonement, the suffering of Christ was looked upon as a satisfaction made to God. Dale, however, abandons this interpretation and affirms that it is God Himself who "endured the penalty instead of inflicting it." Or, as he says in his introduction, "I prefer to recognize in the great Sufferer for mankind the original Moral Ruler of the race."[19]

Much modern discussion in the West has attempted to weave a middle course between an exclusively objective view and an exclusively subjective view. But by and large, like that of R.W. Dale, the discussions have been carried on within the context of the legal mentality that we have seen to be present from the second century onward. Hence the usual attempts to establish an objective interpretation of atonement have gravitated toward the penal view.

---

17. Dale, *The Atonement*, 61.

18. Franks, *The Work of Christ*, 688.

19. *The Atonement*, 63–64. Obviously influenced by Dale, Forsythe emphasizes the same point: "The Christ that we trust all to is not one who died to witness for God, but one in whom God died for His own witness, . . . God was in Christ reconciling. The prime doer in Christ's cross was God. Christ was God reconciling. He was God doing the very best for man, and not man doing his very best before God" (*Cruciality of the Cross*, 17).

There has re-emerged in the twentieth century a completely different alternative that provides a way of speaking of the work of Christ as an objective event that does not involve a change in God's attitude or result in an unsatisfactory substitution of an innocent victim in place of the guilty. It furthermore moves the discussion outside the realm of law. This proposal is associated with the name of Swedish theologian Gustav Aulén who claims that the view he espouses is really a return to a more ancient view to which he refers as the classical theory. He titles this view, *Christus Victor*.

Rather than arguing that the work of Christ effected a change in God's attitude or action, he is suggesting that it effected a change in the situation that was as fully an objective event as the other but with Arminian implications. McGrath remarks, "Aulén offered an approach to the meaning of the death of Christ which by-passed the difficulties of legal approaches, yet vigorously defended the objective nature of the atonement."[20]

Preparatory to advancing his own thesis, Aulén offers some telling criticisms of the satisfaction theories (he calls them Latin views) highlighting their weaknesses. Proponents of the satisfaction theory have often argued that this is the only view that takes sin seriously. However Aulén offers a powerful response to this point: "If God can be represented as willing to accept a satisfaction for sins committed, it appears to follow necessarily that the dilemma of laxity or satisfaction does not adequately express God's enmity against sin. The doctrine provides for the remission of the punishment due to sins, but not for the taking away of the sin itself."[21]

In addition he has pressed the criticism that the Latin theory is not wholly the work of God. Although it begins with God, it is the work of Christ as a man that offers satisfaction to God's justice. In this view, the legal order is uninterrupted, but the order of love is interrupted. This point implies further that in the Latin view, the incarnation and atonement are not organically connected. The purpose of the incarnation is to provide a perfect manhood to offer to God as an acceptable satisfaction.[22] In fact, it "always involves an opposition, expressed or implied, between the Incarnation and the work of Christ."[23] In the light of our concern, Aulén finds that the incarnation and the atonement are organically connected together in the classical view.[24]

---

20. McGrath, *Christian Theology*, 399.
21. *Christus Victor*, 92.
22. Ibid., 87ff., 146.
23. Ibid., 19.
24. Ibid., 87.

In a succinct summary of the contrast between the two interpretations, Aulén says: "The classic idea shows a continuity in the Divine action, and a discontinuity in the order of justice; the Latin type, a legal consistency and a discontinuity in Divine operation."[25]

Aulén's own summary of the classic idea is as follows:

> This type of view may be described provisionally as the "dramatic." Its central theme is the idea of the atonement as a divine conflict and victory; Christ—*Christus Victor*—fights against and triumphs over the evil powers of the world, the "tyrants" under which mankind is in bondage and suffering, and in Him God reconciles the world to Himself.[26]

John Henry Newman's classic lines also reflect this vision:

> Oh, loving wisdom of our God!
> When all was sin and shame.
> A Second Adam to the fight,
> And to the Rescue came.

Aulén professes to only be presenting a historical study and proposes to find this view espoused particularly by Luther. While many feel that he has failed to make his case that it was central to the German reformer (see above on Luther), the *Christus Victor* theme can be better defended by exploring its consistency with the central motif of New Testament theology.

One key term that needs to be defined in exploring the soteriological teachings of biblical theology is "salvation." From its first definitive use in Exodus 14:13, 30, this term carries the connotation of *deliverance*. It means, "to be wide, to be spacious, to be free." This meaning persists throughout the Old Testament, although it is usually viewed with nationalistic overtones. When Israel is in bondage, they look for a savior to deliver them and when God sends a savior or otherwise effects deliverance, they have been saved.

Throughout Israel's history, the struggle for freedom goes on with but temporary and limited success. Ultimately, their unfaithfulness to the covenant relation (sin) results in a return to Egypt in the form of the Babylonian Captivity in 587/86 BC It is out of this history of recurrent periods of slavery that hope arises for a deliverance (salvation) that will be more complete and permanent and with more spiritual overtones. The

---

25. Ibid., 91.
26. Ibid., 4.

structure of the book of Ezekiel reflects the conditions that will be necessary before this can become a reality.

The ministry of Ezekiel is divided into two phases. In the first he is announcing the inevitable destruction of Jerusalem because of her sin. In the second, after the fall of the holy city, he is encouraging the exiles in Babylon by casting a vision of a new day of salvation in which the glory of God will return to his people. The book itself is divided into three sections with a series of oracles of judgment against foreign nations sandwiched between the sections that correspond to the two phases of his ministry. The purpose of this center section depicts the necessary conditions for the reestablishing of the new Israel.

Throughout her history, as noted above, Israel had been prevented from enjoying a free and independent status by these and other foreign powers that had limited her. Thus before she could be saved and experience the position she desired, these hindering obstacles had to be removed. That is the purpose for the oracles announcing the destruction of those nations that surrounded Israel.

The theological understanding that informs this structure reflects the nature of salvation as deliverance from dominating forces, generally seen in the Old Testament as national or political in nature. This concept doubtless also informs some of the early paeans of praise surrounding the birth of Jesus. This same theology is transformed in the New Testament where the BC word is re-theologized into an AD word. As George Eldon Ladd puts it: "The enemies of God's Kingdom are now seen not as hostile evil nations as in the Old Testament but spiritual powers of evil."[27]

To grasp the full significance of this statement, one needs to be aware of the eschatological dualism that marked much of Rabbinic theology in Jesus' day. After a long period of failure to see the fulfillment of the pre-exilic promises of the messianic age, with repeated frustrations created by unfilled hopes, many had given up hope that the kingdom could come within history. This situation gave rise to a literature that looked for the kingdom to come when God would break into history, destroying the social order accompanied by cosmic disturbances, and set up his kingdom. This pessimism about the present was accompanied by the belief that the *present age* was under the control of demonic powers with Satan as the prince of the powers of the air. These powers, including Satan himself, would have to be destroyed before the present age could be delivered from bondage and the *age to come* become a reality.

---

27. Ladd, *A Theology of the New Testament*, 65.

It is the clear teaching of the Synoptic Gospels that the *age to come* had broken into history in the person of Jesus of Nazareth and even though the expected outward manifestations had not occurred, the Kingdom of God had become a present reality in the Christ event. His miracles, especially the exorcisms, were evidences that a power greater than the demonic powers were present.

According to Luke, Jesus launched his ministry at Nazareth by quoting from Isaiah 61—"The Spirit of the Lord is upon Me, Because He has anointed Me to preach the gospel to the poor. He has sent Me to heal the brokenhearted, *To preach deliverance to the captives* And recovery of sight to the blind, To set at liberty those who are oppressed, To preach the acceptable year of the Lord" (vv. 18–19, NKJV, emphasis added). The context of the Isaiah passage is the Babylonian Captivity and the message is addressed to those captives announcing the good news that deliverance (salvation) is coming.

Ladd raises an interesting question. "Why can the victory over evil be won only on the plane of history?" This is tantamount to asking the question of Anselm, *Cur deus homo*? He responds: "No explanation is given, but the answer lies in the fact that the fate of human beings is involved in this struggle. In some way beyond human comprehension, Jesus wrestled with the powers of evil, won a victory over them, that in the end of the age these powers may be finally and forever broken."[28] One might furthermore add that the real existential question of the time (and today as well) is whether or not God can deliver from the power of sin *in this life and history*. Deliverance in the world to come is one thing, but what about the possibility under the conditions of existence. The incarnation, and through it the victory over sin, evil, Satan and death, answer with a resounding affirmative. This is what is meant by the Wesleyan optimism of grace.

This brief survey of New Testament theology should be sufficient to demonstrate that the *Christus Victor* motif is simply the articulation of the central theological understanding that informs the entire New Testament as many New Testament theologians have affirmed.

Many people have discounted this interpretation as being irrelevant to the modern scientific age because its form reflects a mythology that makes no sense to the modern mind. However, as a result of a widespread disenchantment with the Enlightenment worldview, recent years have seen an extensive recognition of the truth of the demonic in human life so that it certainly makes sense at this time in history.

28. Ibid.

In his critique of the exemplarist theory advocated by Hastings Rashdall, Alister McGrath points out that at the same time Rashdall was delivering his Bampton lectures in 1915, a new period in Christian theology was being ushered in by World War I:

> . . . as the naïve bourgeois idealism, so characteristic of the nineteenth century, collapsed in the face of the reality of human evil . . . The effect of such events was to persuade many that the root of man's spiritual problems lay far deeper than mere ignorance, but was grounded in an inherent bias toward evil. Thus the most appropriate analogy for the human condition and the remedy is "that of a man in prison: upon being told that he is in prison, he is not thereby in a significantly better position—he still requires liberation."[29]

In addition to tragic events like World War I, "the insights of Sigmund Freud, which drew attention to the manner in which adults could be spiritually imprisoned by their subconscious, raised serious doubts about the Enlightenment view of the total rationality of human nature, and lent new credibility to the idea that humans are held in bondage to unknown and hidden forces."[30] Even such a sophisticated theologian as Paul Tillich has taken seriously the demonic dimension of existence.[31]

Here, in a word, we have an objective interpretation of the work of Christ that is not a transaction between the Son and the Father, and transcends the legal concerns that many theologians, including myself, feel has sidetracked Western theology from the start but is something that takes place apart from our subjective involvement except as we appropriate the victory won by Christ as our own victory over sin and evil.[32]

---

29. McGrath, "The Moral Theory," 218–19.
30. McGrath, *Christian Theology*, 398.
31. Tillich, *Systematic Theology*, 1:49 et.al.
32. See Greathouse, "Sanctification and the Christus Victor Motif in Wesleyan Theology," 47–59 for a positive assessment of Aulén's thesis vis-à-vis Wesleyan theology. The same journal published a second paper by Greathouse with the same title in Vol. 38, No. 2, Fall, 2003, pp. 217–29.

7

Changing Emphases in Atonement Theology

WHAT WE have seen emerging during the last 100 or so years in the West, as many theologians have worked in increasing interface with scripture, is four-fold:

1. Dissatisfaction with the Traditional Form of the Penal Satisfaction Interpretation of the Work of Christ

Wallace notes that "The beginning of twentieth-century literature on the atonement can be pinpointed to the appearance of James Denney's *The Death of Christ* (1901) and *The Atonement and the Modern Mind* (1903), and R. C. Moberly's *Atonement and Personality* (1901)."[1] Moberly's quite difficult book does little more than adapt John McLeod Campbell's theory of vicarious penitence. More helpful in giving a clue to the changing shape of atonement theologizing is James Denney's work.

His classic work (*The Death of Christ*) seems to be indicative of the direction in which Christian thought in Western theology on the atonement was beginning to move. While typically Western in his focus on the death of Christ, Denney nevertheless recognized that "the starting point of our investigation must be the life and teaching of Jesus Himself."[2] In the light of this principle, he sees the work of atonement as beginning with Jesus' baptism. At this event Jesus numbered himself with the transgressors, "submitting himself to be baptized with their baptism, identifying Himself with them in their relation to God as sinners, making all their responsibilities His own."[3]

In his *Christian Doctrine of Reconciliation*, he highlighted this "new" approach:

---

1. Wallace, *The Work of Christ*, 92.
2. Denney, *The Death of Christ*, 9.
3. Ibid., 21.

> The only incarnation of which the New Testament knows anything is the appearance of Christ in the race and lot of sinful men, and his endurance in it to the end. Apart from sharing our experience, that sharing of our nature, which is sometimes supposed to be what is meant by incarnation, is an abstraction and a figment.[4]

Throughout his work, Denney insists on the propitiatory character of Jesus' death, but unlike the traditional Protestant interpretation of Jesus' death as a sacrifice, he never suggests that his sacrifice was directed toward God but rather reinterprets "propitiation" in terms of "expiation," i.e., having "a reference to sin and its forgiveness."[5] He straightforwardly states that the Old Testament sacrifices

> are looked at simply in the expiatory or atoning significance which is common to them all. They represent a divinely appointed way of dealing with sin, in order that it may not bar fellowship with God; . . . [It is] the conviction of all New Testament Christians that in the death of Christ God has dealt effectually with the world's sin for its removal.[6]

The same point is made by P. T. Forsyth in his lectures given in 1908 and 1909 and published under the title, *The Cruciality of the Cross*. Forsyth declares that his own "point of departure is that Christ's first concern and revelation was not simply the forgiving love of God, but the holiness of such love."[7] One would assume that this emphasis would support some form of a satisfaction interpretation of the death of Christ. But in a concluding chapter on the meaning of "the blood of Christ" he specifically rejects such an idea, saying:

> The positive truth is that the sacrifice is the result of God's grace and not its cause. It is given *by* God before it is given *to* Him. The real ground of any atonement is not in God's wrath but God's grace. There can be no talk of propitiation in the sense of mollification, or of purchasing God's grace, in any religion founded on the Bible.[8]

---

4. Quoted in Hendry, *The Gospel of the Incarnation*, 95.

5. Ibid., 54. Like many others, Denney may be using the terms interchangeably so that the context rather than the term itself will have to determine the meaning. I intend to consistently use "propitiation" to refer to a sacrifice that is directed toward the deity to change his attitude or intention and "expiation" to refer to a sacrifice that is intended to remove the sin that offends the deity.

6. Ibid., 216–17.

7. *The Cruciality of the Cross*, viii.

8. Ibid., 89.

In a most felicitous phrase he nails the issue: "Procured grace is a contradiction in terms."[9]

In his exposition of the Pauline teaching, Denney avoids the misunderstanding that had characterized the liberal theology of the nineteenth century that saw Paul perverting the simple gospel taught by Jesus into a pre-Christian view of propitiation. Paul connected the death of Christ, says Denney, with three realities:

1) To begin with, he defines it in relation to the love of God. ". . . The interpretation of Christ's death through the love of God is fundamental in St. Paul."[10]

2) Further, the apostle defines Christ's death in relation to the love of Christ. Christ is not an instrument, but the agent of the Father in all that He does.

3) The relation of Christ's death to the love of God and of Christ is its fundamental relation on the one side; on the other side, St. Paul relates it essentially to sin.

With regard to the third point, Denney's pivotal thesis is succinctly stated: "Death is the word which sums up the whole liability of man in relation to sin, and therefore when Christ came to give Himself for our sins He did it by dying."[11] The entire mood of Denney's exposition is shaped by the premise that "the work of reconciling is one in which the initiative is taken by God, and the cost borne by Him; men are reconciled in the passive, or allow themselves to be reconciled, or receive the reconciliation. We never read that God has been reconciled."[12]

By following St. Paul in identifying sin and death, Denney avoids the interpretation of satisfaction theories that imputes the sinfulness of mankind to Christ. The scriptures that have been the sources of this interpretation are thus given a sounder interpretation consistent with the whole tenor of scripture.

D. E. H. Whiteley takes a similar approach in interpreting what he calls the "three famous passages [in Paul] which have so often been regarded as foundation stones of the substitution theory—Rom viii. 3–4, 2 Cor v. 21, and Gal iii. 13." He argues that "none of these either necessitate or excludes a substitutionary explanation, and if such a theory were firmly based upon other passages in the Pauline writings it would be legitimate to

---

9. Ibid., 41.
10. Denney, *The Death of Christ*, 124.
11. Ibid., 128.
12. Ibid., 144.

inepret [sic] these three also in a similar manner." But taken as a whole, says Whiteley, "if St. Paul can be said to hold a theory of the *modus operandi*, it is the 'participation' theory: his other sayings are to be regarded as statements of the fact of the atonement, expressed by means of the religious language of Judaism."[13]

The basis of Denney's interpretation is his emphasis on Jesus' complete identification with fallen mankind. "To say that the Son of God was made under the law [Gal 3:13] would thus mean that He had the same moral problem in His life as other men; that He identified Himself with them in the spiritual conditions under which they lived; that the incarnation was a moral reality and not a mere show."[14] Did this bring Him under the curse of sin? Denney answers:

> Christ hung on the tree in obedience to the Father's will, fulfilling the purpose of the Father's love, doing a work with which the Father was well pleased, and on account of which the Father highly exalted Him; hence to describe Him as accursed of God would be absurd. . . Death is the curse of the law. It is the experience in which the final repulsion of evil by God is decisively expressed; and Christ died. In His death everything was made His that sin had made ours—everything in sin except its sinfulness.[15]

The greatest weakness of Denney's treatment is his failure to take with full seriousness Paul's teaching about our identification with Christ, rejecting this teaching as being a "second doctrine of reconciliation."[16] The confusion here is in speaking of it as having to do with salvation in the narrow sense and not recognizing that this aspect of Paul's teaching relates to sanctification (or salvation in the broader sense). He does, however, rightly speak about the new life in Christ as a response to the propitiatory death of Christ and somewhat reluctantly acknowledges the Pauline idea of mystical union with Christ as something which is not a substitute

---

13. Whitely, *The Theology of Paul*, 134ff.

14. Denney, *The Death of Christ*, 155.

15. Ibid., 160.

16. This was apparently a popular view in the nineteenth century that held that "Paul has two doctrines of redemption, one that is juridical (justification) and one of a really new creation by the Spirit, with the first based largely on the Cross, the second largely on the resurrection" (Ziesler, *The Meaning of Righteousness in Paul*, 6). Ziesler adds, "The idea of two distinct soteriologies is now widely rejected, and we also find it unacceptable." The purpose behind such an interpretation was the difficulty of moving from the Protestant view of justification to ethics (sanctification), a view that Ziesler says has been called a "cul-de-sac." This reflects Wesley's chief problem with the satisfaction theory.

for, but the fruit of the vicarious death of Christ.[17] This is, of course, the proper understanding as Denney clearly captures in one comment: "The working in us of the mind of Christ toward sin, which presumably is what is meant by our identification with Him in His death, is not the making of atonement, nor the basis of our reconciliation to God, it is the fruit of the Atonement, which is Christ's finished work."[18] In simple language, this merely states the biblical teaching that we are saved by grace alone and not by our good works, or moral living, (even if imputed) and yet that gracious acceptance calls for a loving response of a holy life. It is clear that Denney has not made a clean break with Western juridical language and concepts but his modifications create a crack in the system that will become wider and wider as the century progressed.

There are, of course, dissenting voices to this move away from orthodoxy, voices that are chiefly within the tradition of Protestant scholasticism. One of the most vocal theologians seeking to defend this tradition is Leon Morris.

Morris generally appears to hang his case on the meaning of certain key terms: redemption, covenant, the blood, propitiation, reconciliation, and justification. In particular, he gives special attention to seeking to demonstrate that the word *hilasterion* means "propitiation" suggesting, as he says, that it is to be understood in terms of the averting of the divine wrath.[19]

He is concerned to establish the absolute objectivity of the atonement and for that reason argues that the sacrifice of Jesus was a propitiation of the wrath of God. He admits that pagan antecedents were capricious and vindictive, yet argues:

> When the term was taken over into the Bible these unworthy and crude ideas were abandoned, and only the central truth expressed by the term was retained, namely that propitiation signifies the averting of wrath by the offering of a gift. But in both the Old Testament and New the thought is plain that the gift which secures the propitiation is from God Himself, he provides the way whereby men may come to him.[20]

This qualification, however, sets up an inherent contradiction. If the source of the provision of a propitiation is the one who is to be propitiated,

---

17. Ibid., 184–85.
18. Ibid., 237.
19. Morris, "The Meaning of *Hilasterion* in Romans 3:24," 33–43.
20. Morris, *The Apostolic Preaching of the Cross*, 129, 183.

there is ultimately no need for it. This is often countered by arguing that the need for propitiation is a duality within God that needs to be resolved. But Hendry's comment shows how this has no scriptural support:

> This conception that forgiveness presents a kind of dilemma to God, who has to devise a way in which he can exercise mercy under the guise of justice, without letting his left hand know what his right hand doeth, is, as we have already noted, completely at variance with the New Testament which nowhere suggests that forgiveness is a problem for God.[21]

The purpose of the death of Christ is certainly more positive and wider-visioned than Morris sees in his explanation of the purpose of the atonement. And if this is how it is to be preached, it will likely have little existential apologetic value in the contemporary world. James S. Stewart's statement that "it cannot be too firmly emphasized that the whole idea of propitiating God is radically unscriptural" more nearly resonates with the whole tenor of scripture.[22]

A much more defensible position is that of T. W. Manson, who argues that *hilasterion* is "a noun denoting the locality at which the acts or events covered by the verb *hilaskesthi* takes place."[23] In a word, it refers to the mercy seat where God and men come together. Even further removed from the so-called orthodox view is the suggestion of James Denney that the term *hilasterion* is not a noun at all, but a masculine adjective agreeing with *hon*—"whom God hath set forth with propitiatory power."[24]

In agreeing with Manson (and C. H. Dodd) on the meaning of *hilasterion*, Whitely highlights the centrality of the concept of redemption that recalls the Exodus and comments about Paul's use of the concept:

> It is God's New Exodus work of salvation, looked for at the end of the ages, now already partially accomplished in Christ Jesus. God through Christ has dealt with sin, and so Christ is called the place where, or the means whereby, sin is dealt with; in him the purpose for which the Mercy Seat (Heb. *kappōreth*, Greek, *hilastērion*) had been intended was perfectly fulfilled. God's new act of redemption in Christ binds us to himself as the Israelites had been bound by

---

21. Hendry, *The Gospel of the Incarnation*, 121.
22. Stewart, *A Man in Christ*, 217.
23. Manson, "Hilasterion," 1–10.
24. Quoted by Stewart, *A Man in Christ*, 215 from *The Expositor's Greek Testament*, ii. 611.

the blood of the Mosaic covenant, and so it is said to have taken place through the blood of Christ.[25]

2. A Somewhat Subtle Recognition of the Pervasive Influence of Hellenistic Modes of Thought on the Doctrine of God

Identifying this perversion of biblical theology has led to an increasing abandonment of the idea of the impassive nature of God and an embracing of the fact of God's passivity, that he is a dynamic reality, including the fact that he suffers. Instead of being a heresy, *patripassionism* has now become a joyfully accepted doctrine by many. This transformation is frequently introduced into discussions about the problem of evil but it also leads to a radically different way of seeing the atonement that has been classically expressed by Donald Baillie in his book, *God was in Christ*.

Unlike those who conceive forgiveness as a good-natured indulgence, Baillie recognizes that forgiveness is a costly reconciliation, not in spite of but because of God's love. "God's love must be inexorable towards our sins; not because He is just, but because He is loving; not in spite of his love, but because of His love; not because His love is limited but because it is unlimited, ..."[26]

While recognizing that analogies from human experience are limited, Baillie seeks to illustrate how God Himself suffers in the process of forgiveness and reconciliation by the example of a disruptions of relations between close friends. Perhaps an even stronger analogy might be an act of infidelity by a marriage partner. The one who has been wronged is the one who has the hardest part to play in reconciliation. "It is he who bears the brunt. He suffers more than I. Not because he is the person that has been wronged: nay, it is the shame of what I have done that weighs most on him. He bears my shame as if it were his own, because of his great love for me. He bears more of the agony than I." When we recognize that only God knows us perfectly and loves us most completely, we are able to see the infinite suffering involved in his forgiveness. "Our reconciliation is infinitely costly to Him. Not in the sense that it is difficult for Him to forgive us, as it would be difficult for a Shylock, who has to be induced not to insist upon

---

25. Whitely, *The Theology of Paul*, 146.
26. Baillie, *God was in Christ*, 173.

his pound of flesh . . . There is an atonement, an expiation, in the heart of God Himself, and out of this comes the forgiveness of our sins."[27]

There are really only two options if sins are to be forgiven and reconciliation is to be actualized. Either we must bear our sins or God must bear them. St. Paul, in his own experience, demonstrated the impossibility of the former out of which grew his understanding of unconditional grace. But perhaps another man can bear our sins in our stead. Our earlier analyzes showed that this was what Anselm and Calvin had in mind in their answer to the question, *Cur Deus Homo*. But our survey of the history of atonement theology has demonstrated that perceptive theologians have shown that there are insuperable barriers to this even though these classic interpretations of the atonement have argued that it was Christ as man that bore our sins and rendered satisfaction to God. The only other option available then is for God himself to bear our sins and we believe it is the most proper interpretation of the New Testament to see that in the death of Christ, this is precisely what is being manifested.

In 1 Corinthians 15:17 Paul says, "And if Christ has not been raised, your faith is futile; you are still in your sins." What can he mean by this? We are accustomed to his argument that apart from the resurrection of Christ we are without hope so far as a postmortem future is concerned but how does the resurrection provide hope for the forgiveness of sins? If we view the crucifixion as God in Christ bearing our sins, the resurrection is God's good housekeeping seal of approval that this has indeed occurred. Just as the resurrection validates Jesus' transformation of the messianic hope by the Suffering Servant ideal, so it validates his being the sin-bearer, not as a man taking our place, but as God himself bearing the cost of reconciliation.

If we take the whole Christ event as definitive of the atonement, we have a significant support for this position. If indeed "in Christ God was reconciling the world to himself" (2 Cor 5:19) the divine attitude and activity is most clearly reflected in that of Jesus. Karl Barth has pointed out the peculiar manner in which the Greek verb *splagchnizesthai* is applied to Jesus in the Gospels (cf. Mt 9:36; 14:14; 20:34; Luke 7:13, et. al.). The word, derived from *splagchna*, "the nobler visera," denotes an emotion that penetrates to the inmost depths of one's being, and for which "to have mercy" or "compassion" is too weak a rendering. When referred to Jesus, it means, as Barth said it, that

---

27. Ibid., 174–75.

the pain, the sin, the absolutely forlorn and desperate condition of these men and this people not only affected Jesus, not only touched his heart, but so entered into his heart, into his very self, that all this misery was now in him and became his own misery, and as such was much more acutely realized and more painfully felt by him than by them; *esplagchnisthei* means: he took this misery upon himself, he took it away from them and made it his own affair, his own misery."[28]

Evidently, Charles Wesley glimpsed the light of this truth in his memorable lines:

> And can it be that I should gain
> An int'rest in the Savor's blood?
> Died he for me who caused His pain?
> For me who Him to death pursued?
> Amazing love, how can it be
> *That Thou My God shouldst die for me!*
> (Emphasis added)

3. Use of Personal Categories

A further emphasis that we noticed is a growing recognition of the inadequacy of a juridical or legalistic way of interpreting the atonement accompanied by a turn to the personal dimension as the decisive context within which the work of Christ can be best interpreted. As Donald Baillie put it, "In theological argument on this subject we are apt to forget that we are dealing with a realm of personal relationships and nothing else."[29]

P. T. Forsyth, in commenting on the metaphysical language of the creeds, notes that

> most of those theories were fastened on the Church in the interest, indeed, of a true redemption, but at a time when the theology of redemption, was apt to be conceived in terms of substance rather than subject, of metaphysic rather than ethic, of things rather than persons . . . But we have come to a time in the growth of Christian moral culture when personal relations and personal movements count for more than the relations of the most rare and ethereal substances.[30]

---

28. Barth, *Church Dogmatics*, III.2, 252, quoted in Hendry, *The Gospel of the Incarnation*, 102–3.

29. Baillie, *God was in Christ*, 198.

30. Forsyth, *The Person and Place of Jesus Christ*, 331f.

The emphasis on the personal in post-modern thought is at the same time an emphasis on "relation" as the viable way to deal with theological matters. In attempting to articulate the atonement in terms relevant to this way of thinking, Alan Mann says: ". . . even taking Pauline interpretation into account, a biblical understanding of atonement is concerned above all with the restoration of mutual, undistorted, unpolluted divine/human relationship, not with the appeasing of a God angered by the misdeeds of his creatures."[31]

This move by some theologians appears in terms of a return to the classic Reformers, Luther and Calvin, whose emphasis on the personal element in religion tended to be obscured in Protestant orthodoxy. George Hendry notes this shift:

> When Luther spoke of justification by faith, he meant faith in Christ; but to many of his successors it came to mean faith in justification. It is significant that in the theology of Lutheran orthodoxy the personal relation to Christ, the "mystical union," was isolated and set at a distance from justification in the plan of salvation (*ordo salutis*). The same tendency is apparent in the Reformed [Calvinistic] branch of Protestantism, where faith often came to mean faith in the Bible. In both, faith was a doctrinaire, propositional affair rather than a living personal relationship; and the piety, which was regulated by this faith, tended to become a cold, hard, formal thing. It is no wonder, therefore, that a recurring feature of Protestant history has been what we may call the revolt of piety against faith; *for piety cannot thrive in the context of an impersonal and propositional faith; it seeks attachment to the person of Christ.*[32]

This latter point has been reinforced by the insistence of many that the central soteriological concept of the New Testament is reconciliation. In fact, as Baillie notes, "A great deal of confusion has been caused by the fact that the English word 'atonement' has moved away from the sense it had when the Bible was translated, viz., reconciliation."[33] Alister McGrath verifies that William Tyndale introduced it into theological vocabulary as an equivalent to reconciliation.[34] Reconciliation is a metaphor derived from the realm of personal relations. However, to say this does not really set reconciliation in opposition to justification, when the latter term is

---

31. Mann, *Atonement for a "Sinless" Society*, 94.
32. Hendry, *The Gospel of the Incarnation*, 18, emphasis added.
33. Baillie, *God was in Christ*, 187.
34. McGrath, "The Moral Theory," 205.

properly understood scripturally, so that we are to choose been two contrary teachings (see below).

The personal context enables us to understand the *must* of Jesus, what theologically we have referred to as the necessity of the atonement. This is a crucial issue, as James Denney emphasized. He says, "The one point in which all the narratives agree is that Jesus taught that He *must* go up to Jerusalem and die; and the one question it is of importance to answer is, What is meant by this *must* (dei)?"[35]

Too often the emphasis on the necessity of the death of Christ makes God subservient to a law above himself rather than grounded in the very nature of God itself. The ambiguity of the term "necessity" when applied to the suffering of the Savior has resulted in tremendous confusion about the meaning and significance of the cross. Martin Luther said, "Necessity belongs to 'physics,' not theology. If this concept is to be used in theology we must 'bathe and wash it.'"[36] Unfortunately Luther did not use sufficiently strong soap.

"Necessity" derives its meaning from the context. There is a legal necessity, a moral necessity, a logical necessity, and a legitimate concept of necessity that arises out of personal relations. It is from this latter context that the concept should be derived when speaking about the *must* that was the driving force behind Jesus' movement toward the cross. There is a necessary suffering involved in the restoration of broken personal relations (see above on the abandonment of the idea of the passivity of God).

Vincent Taylor voices the modern conscience when he says: "Gone for ever are feudal and merely legal conceptions of God, except in quarters where the modern spirit finds it difficult to enter. In fact, our danger is that of being content with this great truth, deepened by a growing emphasis upon the suffering of God Himself, and by the claim that the love is objectively manifested."[37]

Another important concept contributing to the emphasis on the personal is the recognition of the nature of covenant. This is a pervasive theme throughout the scripture and a case can be made that covenant is the unifying motif of the Bible.[38] It's importance for our subject is seen in the fact that at the Last Supper with his disciples, Jesus identified what was

---

35. Denney, *The Death of Christ*, 29.
36. Quoted in Johnson, *The Humanity of the Saviour*, 28.
37. Taylor, *The Doctrine of the Atonement*, 195.
38. Cf. Eichrodt, *Theology of the Old Testament*.

about to occur in the climax of his ministry as the establishment of the new covenant.

The point at issue, which biblical theologians have now come to see, is that a covenant is to be distinguished from a contract. The former is personal in nature while the latter is legal. According to Robert Letham, the covenant came to be regarded as a contract during the Reformation period under the influence of Roman law.[39] A contract is characteristically thing-oriented whereas the covenant is person-oriented. When speaking theologically, the covenant "arises, not with benefits as the chief barter item, but out of a desire for a measure of intimacy."[40] The marriage relation is perhaps the most fruitful analogy with the biblical covenant and is frequently so used in the Scripture.[41]

In a discussion of the nature of sin in the eighth century prophets, Norman Snaith insists that their view of sin is religious rather than ethical and that this has been widely misunderstood due to the way English translations have rendered the Hebrew word *peshà* as "transgression," suggesting violation of a code of laws whereas for the prophets, it really carried the meaning of rebellion. To this point he comments: "The equation [sin as rebellion] is not surprising when we remember that before the Exile the covenant was thought of entirely as a personal relationship towards Jehovah, the idea of a written law being a later and mostly post-exilic idea."[42]

4. Recognition of the Corporate Nature of Biblical Faith

In more recent theological work, the idea of solidarity appears with increasing frequency accompanied by a questioning of the individualism that has become so dominant in the West.[43] While it is clearly the case that this teaching has not filtered down to the rank and file of American evangelicals, theologians and biblical scholars have all but unanimously recognized that this individualism is foreign to biblical modes of thought. Solidarity does not depend upon a Platonic ontology, but upon the biblical understanding of the nature of personhood as being social and relational

---

39. Letham, *The Work of Christ*, 40.

40. Martens, *God's Design*, 73.

41. See also Torrance, "Covenant or Contract?" 51–76.

42. Snaith, *Distinctive Ideas of the Old Testament*, 63. This observation does not necessarily depend upon certain critical views about the dating of Old Testament material as reflected in Snaith's statement.

43. Cf. Whiteley, *The Theology of St. Paul*, 45–46.

in nature. In the language of John MacMurray's classic Gifford Lectures, we are "persons in relation."[44] In terms of technical theology, this move may seem on the surface to support the *anhypostasia* teaching of Cyril of Alexandria, which became generally accepted in the Western church. The problem with this solution is that it depends on Platonic ontology, which no longer has currency philosophically. Rather, the incarnation means that the Word became an individual human being (not a generic human) but was the perfect embodiment of the image of God which is a relational concept and so stands in a relation of solidarity with the human race.

William Temple made a well-known classic statement in his Gifford Lectures in which he described the day on which Descartes conceived his *cogito ergo sum* as the most disastrous day in the history of philosophical thought.[45] It is now generally recognized that personal being is essentially being in relation, not being in isolation; no longer as a circle with "I" at the center; it has become an ellipse with two foci, "I and Thou."

---

44. MacMurray, *Persons in Relation*, and *The Self as Agent*.
45. Temple, *Nature, Man and God*, 57.

8

Insights from Biblical Theology

In Protestant Scholasticism the Bible was generally used as a repository of proof-texts to support the prevailing dogmatic systems. With the emancipation of the scripture from this subservient role the way was opened for God's word to be heard on its own terms. The emergence of the discipline of biblical theology in the early twentieth century as an "inductive, descriptive discipline, synthetic in approach, which on the basis of a grammatico-historical study of the Biblical text seeks to set forth in its own terms and in its structural unity the theology expressed in the Bible"[1] became the occasion for many new theological insights that had been unnoticed under the older use of scripture. Some of these impact the paradigm in terms of which the work of Christ should be interpreted. In this chapter we propose to explore some of these to support our thesis that the best paradigm is a personal-relational one.

The Meaning of Justification

One of the most important aspects of recent studies in biblical theology is the emergence of a more adequate Biblical understanding of justification, which many Biblical scholars now see to be primarily a covenant word. Actually, the basic term is *righteousness*, justification being more properly translated by the awkward term *righteousfication*. In this light it is significant that "the general context in which righteousness is always used in the Old Testament is the context of the Covenant."[2] Much confusion has occurred in the history of Christian theologizing about soteriology through a failure to recognize this meaning. But it is understandable that this has occurred since the terms *tsedheq* and *tsedhaqah* have multiple meanings. Therefore as Bollier says, "Because the origin of this word is so obscure and the possibility for the word to change its meaning in the course of usage is

---

1. Bright, *The Authority of the Old Testament*, 114–15.
2. Bollier, "The Righteousness of God," 404–13.

so likely, it is best to seek the meaning of *sedheq* and its cognates in their specific contexts."[3]

The major issue throughout the history of Christian thought has been whether justification means *to make righteous* or *to declare righteous*. The former position, early on adopted by St. Augustine, became largely the Catholic view whereas the latter was the dominant Protestant emphasis. The problem is that both of these views have historically understood "righteousness" as ethical, or legal uprightness.[4]

This legal perspective has been such a pervasive element that even good scholars seem to be unaware of the fallacy involved. For instance, when writing about atonement and justification Robert Letham says:

> We must remember that in discussing justification we are concerned with the situation of a law court, an objective and forensic matter. What is at stake is the question of our status before God in terms of his law. By his sin, Adam plunged the race into guilt. We had infringed God's righteous and holy law and were guilty before God.[5]

The fallacy here, according to N. T. Wright, is not in identifying the law court as the context for the biblical meaning of justification, but conceiving the law court in the mode of Western retributive justice whereas the concept is informed by the Jewish law court, which is dramatically different. Here, all cases consist of an accuser and a defendant, there being no public prosecutor. The judge upholds the case of one party in the dispute and that person is justified and is described as just. This simply describes his status before the court, not his moral character. Things are put right.[6]

Bernhard W. Anderson, in discussing the meaning of righteousness in the Psalms says, "In facing this question we should divest ourselves of notions of righteousness that we have inherited from our culture, largely under Greek and Roman influence. Normally we assume that a 'righteous' person is one who conforms to some legal or moral standard. Such person is held to be righteous according to the law."[7]

---

3. Ibid.

4. Cf. Forde, "The Exodus from Virtue to Grace: Justification by Faith Today," 32–44. "The old argument about whether we are only 'declared' righteous or actually 'made' so is largely beside the point. It presupposes that our schemes remain intact."

5. *The Work of Christ*, 178.

6. N. T. Wright, "Justification."

7. Anderson, *Out of the Depths*, 100–101.

Insights from Biblical Theology

Interpreting justification in the light of righteousness understood ethically or legally resulted in the explanations of both Catholic and classical Protestant views mentioned above, both of which John Wesley explicitly rejected. The first because it confuses justification with sanctification and the second because it is based on a legal fiction, where God treats the believer as righteous even though she/he is not.

Perhaps inadvertently, Wesley anticipated more recent discoveries in biblical theology by his distinction between justification as *a relative change*, and sanctification as *a real change*. As Ziesler comments, "Although it is often acknowledged that elsewhere *dikaiosuna* may have an ethical meaning, in 'justification' contexts a relational meaning is . . . widely accepted."[8]

There appears to be four major uses of the righteousness vocabulary. One refers, as noted, to ethical righteousness and this is the most popular understanding in the contemporary use of the term. Another, applied primarily to God, refers to *faithfulness to one's word*. This implies a promise and if one manifests fidelity to that promise, he or she is considered "righteous." A third is also attributed primarily to God and found its enacted meaning expressed in the Exodus where Yahweh came to the aid of an enslaved people and delivered them on the basis of his compassion. Thus righteousness suggests compassion or mercy toward the needy and helpless. It is this third meaning that Martin Luther discovered in his studies of Romans that became the basis of his Copernican revolution in soteriology. The *righteousness of God* was not, as in Catholic piety, the ethical righteousness God requires as a prerequisite to accepting us, a righteousness Luther felt he could never achieve, but God's own attitude of grace and mercy toward helpless, sinful mankind.

Each of these three meanings has significance for a full-orbed doctrine of the atonement, but the fourth is of critical importance for a proper understanding of justification. "Righteousness" here is a personal, relational, covenantal term. *In this context, a person is considered righteous when he or she conforms to the requirements of the relation within which they stand.* The classical illustration of this use is found in Genesis 38 in the sordid story of Tamar and Judah. The covenantal context of this story is the Levirate law regarding marriage. If a man marries and dies without offspring, his brother is to marry his widow and rear at least the first child for his brother's heir. Judah's son married Tamar and died with no child whereupon Judah gave her his second son for husband. But he refused to carry out his prescribed role and died as a result. Judah refused to give Tamar the third son on the excuse that he was too young. But with the passing of time, it became

---

8. Ziesler, *The Meaning of Righteousness*, 9.

clear that Judah did not intend to fulfill his promise. Therefore Tamar took matters into her own hands, disguised herself as a prostitute, seduced her father-in-law and became pregnant by him. When Judah discovered his daughter-in-law was with child he was righteously indignant! But upon discovering that he was the father, he declared Tamar *to be more righteous than himself* (Gen 38:26). She had kept the terms of the covenant and he had not. She was therefore righteous relationally even though ethical righteousness was far away.[9]

The central paradigm for its soteriological use in scripture is found in Genesis 15.[10] The key is verse 6—"And [Abram] believed the Lord and the Lord reckoned it to him as righteousness." The elements of a covenant-making encounter are all here. There is the promise from God to provide Abram a son of his own and subsequently innumerable descendents. Abram's part of the covenant was simply to believe God and therefore by believing he was declared righteous. There is no mention of Abram's ethical character and qualifications. That was irrelevant in this particular case.

This covenant between Yahweh and Abram was consummated by a sacrifice that had unique features. Abram was to provide several sacrificial animals and birds, sever them into halves (except the smallest) and place them in a position to provide a corridor between the halves. Some scholars believe that the term *berith*, translated as "covenant," literally means "to cut a covenant." If this is accurate it is certainly appropriate here.

In usual practice the covenant partners would apparently pass between the halves of the slaughtered animals thereby declaring their intention to keep the promises made to each other. The symbolism said that if they did not keep their word, they were willing that their destiny be that of the sacrifices. In this case, only God (symbolized by the smoking fire pot and the flaming torch) passed through the corridor thus pledging his own extinction if he did not keep his promise to Abram. God placed conditions upon himself, Abram's only condition was faith. On these grounds the patriarch could be counted as righteous *relationally* because he met his part of the covenant requirements, he believed (trusted) God. In a word he was justified (righteousified) by faith. Anderson states it plainly, "The righteousness accounted to him [Abram] was being in right relationship with God, as shown by his trust in God's promise even when there was no evidence to support it—none but the myriads of stars in the sky!"[11]

---

9. See an excellent discussion of this in Ladd, *Theology of the New Testament*, 480–81.
10. Cf. Romans 4:1–25.
11. Anderson, *Out of the Depths*, 101.

One major theological debate arising out of the failure to recognize the covenantal meaning of righteousness directly impinges on how one views the atonement. This debate concerns the issues of the meaning and relation between *imputed* and *imparted* righteousness. Standard Protestant textbooks have spent much time distinguishing between these and arguing for one or the other, depending on the theologian's point of view. Imputed righteousness refers to the righteousness of Christ credited to the account of the believer whereas imparted righteousness suggests that the believer is truly sanctified or really righteous in himself, even if conceived as a gift (as Augustine).

In the light of the understanding of righteousness here discussed the whole complex of issues surrounding the debate disappears, since both positions assume the necessity of ethical righteousness as a requirement for God's acceptance. With that interpretation now cleared up, the issue is a moot point.

The question of whether the term "justification" means to make holy or simply to declare holy is also addressed by this view. If God declares a person righteous in the relational sense, that declaration makes it true, not as a legal fiction, but in a real, though nonethical, sense. It is on this basis that one may refer to justification as a forensic term but having none of the denotations traditionally attached to the term as suggesting declaring a person righteous in opposition to his or her actual character.

When one takes the multiple meanings of righteousness and attempts to allow the context to determine which meaning is intended, St. Paul's discussions about justification assume a look quite different from much traditional understanding. Thereby much tortured exegesis can be avoided, especially with the Epistle to the Romans.

In a survey of the righteousness vocabulary in Romans, Ziesler argues that there is continual interplay between the forensic (meaning to declare righteous relationally, as above) and the ethical meaning. This reflects the struggle by the apostle to avoid the implication that justification by grace through faith alone that puts a person right with God implies antinomianism but actually calls for ethical transformation. John Wesley's continued emphasis that sanctification really begins in justification may suggest this same paradoxical relation since he insists on avoiding confusing the two.[12]

Whiteley recognizes the proper relation between these two meanings in his note that "Justification (*dikaiosune*; Heb. *tsedhakah*) is to be regarded as a regal rather than a juridical word. It means neither to make ethically righteous, which we are not, nor to account righteous by a legal

---

12. Cf. Outler, *Theology in the Wesleyan Spirit*, 52.

fiction, but to set in a right relationship with God, a relationship by virtue of which sanctification can proceed."[13]

Norman Snaith makes essentially the same observation concerning Paul's use of the term suggesting that he inherited both views (ethical and relational) from the Old Testament, He says:

> He [Paul] uses the noun in the double sense, sometimes in a truly ethical sense and sometimes practically as the equivalent of salvation. When he writes of the law of righteousness (Rom 9:31), he is referring to the ethical demands of the Mosaic law, but when he uses the phrase "the righteousness of God," he means that salvation which God accomplishes through Christ (Rom 3:21).[14]

The covenant ceremony that established the relation between Yahweh and Abram also provides us with a revolutionary insight into the meaning of sacrifice in the Old Testament. This meaning then will inform our understanding of how to properly interpret the references to the work of Christ that use sacrificial imagery.[15] Very few scholars have seemed to recognize that there is a difference between sacrifices that are involved in establishing a covenant relation and those that function within the covenant relation to maintain the relation. Confusion between these two has resulted in imbalanced views of the sacrifice of Christ.[16]

In the covenant establishing sacrifices, the point at issue seems to be the promises that are warranted by the ritual. As with the Abrahamic covenant, there is not the slightest hint of an offering to placate or propitiate God but in a very real sense the symbolism points to the fact that God is employing the symbol of sacrifice as a promise to keep his word, that is, to be righteous.

The human covenant partner is simply called upon to believe (trust) the promise. In cases like the sacrifice connected with the Passover, the recipients of the promise need to act out their faith by applying the blood to the lentils and door posts of their home. But this action is basically an acted response of faith in the promise. Whiteley says "the Passover blood was a means of salvation, and it was not regarded anywhere in the Old

13. Whiteley, *The Theology of Paul*, 141.

14. Snaith, "Righteousness."

15. The assumption behind this statement is that the continuity between the Old and New Testaments is to be found in the theological content of each. Even though the BC word is retheologized into an AD word by the New, the theological structure remains the same. In my opinion the most important presentation of this position is John Bright, *The Authority of the Old Testament*.

16. Culpepper, *Interpreting the Atonement* is a notable exception.

Testament as being expiatory or propitiatory, although such ideas would appear to have been associated with it in later Jewish thought."[17]

What are the implications of this relational view of justification for the atonement? When the concept is removed from the Western courtroom and placed in a personal context, the entire situation is changed. We are no longer faced with the dilemma of punishment or laxity. Rather we see God in Christ freely, not reluctantly, offering forgiveness to the rebellious sinner but at a tremendous cost to himself. The question that always presents itself is the extent of the offer of forgiveness. While the promises of scripture, both Old and New Testaments, are universal, to *whosoever will*, the Christ event culminating in the laying down his life at the Cross is an enacted, implicit promise that the provision is inclusive. When he died with his arms outstretched, as Athanasius put it, he embraced all mankind.[18] And as with all promises, the proper response is trust or faith. *Thus the promise-faith correlation stands at the heart of the atonement.*

Apart from this inclusive promise, there is no possibility of Christian assurance. Faith could never rise above the level of uncertain hope. But in the light of the cross as God's universal provision for all human persons, no one can ever look at the crucifixion and doubt that "he died for *me*."

The Meaning of Sacrifice

We have opened up the question of the meaning of sacrifice in the discussion of justification. It seems appropriate to round out that issue at this point. The meaning of sacrifice is one of the most debated questions in biblical theology. Unfortunately, there is no rationale explicitly given in the Old Testament itself. One is left to draw conclusions about its meaning from a broader base that would include the practice itself, its contrast with pagan use and such passages of scripture as might impinge, albeit indirectly, on the matter.

The importance of the theological significance of covenant establishing sacrifices is seen in the fact that Jesus' celebration of the Passover with his disciples was accompanied by his announcement that it was a portent of a New Covenant that would be inaugurated by his death. W. D. Davies argues that Paul's meaning in his eucharistic passage (1 Cor 15:23; 5:7) is also that the paschal lamb symbolized the institution of a covenant:

---

17. Whiteley, *The Theology of Paul*, 140.
18. Athanasius, *On the Incarnation*, c. 25.

> Just as in the Jewish Passover we have a memorial festival of thanksgiving for a past event that had led to the formation of the community of the old Israel so for Paul the Death of Jesus, when he thinks of the Eucharist, is primarily the means whereby the New Community is constituted . . . It is not then as sacrificial and expiatory but as covenantal that Paul chiefly thinks of the Death of Jesus in the context of the Last Supper, although of course everything covenantal had a sacrificial basis.[19]

The second function of sacrifice takes place *within* the covenant relation. It was a cultic ritual performed by the people of God. To the extent that it has an atoning significance, it may be referred to as functioning to maintain the covenant relation. The primary biblical source for our knowledge of these sacrifices is Leviticus 1–7, clearly defining cultic rituals.[20]

Several extremely important considerations must be taken into account. First, these sacrifices only cover *inadvertent* sins. There is no sacrifice for willful or *high-handed* sin. According to Numbers 15:30 such sins result in the expulsion of the offender from the community. He is placed outside the camp symbolizing his removal from the sphere of salvation which is within the community of faith.

A second question relates to how the sin offering (*hattath*) functions. Is it propitiatory or expiatory?[21] The solution partly hangs on how the term *hilasmos* is interpreted, an issue we have earlier discussed. It is clear from scholarly studies that propitiation is the rationale for pagan sacrifices. While one cannot *a priori* deny that that is also the purpose of Israelite sacrifices, on the surface it seems unlikely that there would be a theological continuity with paganism at this point when there is a distinct discontinuity at every other point including numerous directives in the Old Testament for God's people to dissociate themselves from pagan practices.[22]

---

19. Davies, *Paul and Rabbinic Judaism*, 252.

20. The sin offering and the trespass offering are the ones primarily relevant to this discussion.

21. In order to be fair, we will allow one who supports the "propitiation" interpretation to define the terms: "By 'propitiation' we mean that element of the work of Christ directed towards God by which the wrath and condemnation of God resting on guilty man is removed and the way is opened for God to receive man into fellowship with Himself . . . In expiation man's sin is the object of the action, whereas in propitiation God Himself is the object. Something takes place in relation to God, which makes it possible for Him to remove His sentence of judgment against men and to receive them into fellowship with Himself. *Sin* is expiated, but *God* is propitiated." Connell, "The Propitiatory Element in the Atonement," 28.

22. Connell (see previous note) correctly recognizes that the nature of God is the

Robert Culpepper, following a careful discussion of this issue concludes:

> The fact that it is God himself who covers the sin is the basic difference in the understanding of sacrifice manifested in the Old Testament as compared with that in heathen religions. It is God himself who manifests his grace to man in providing a means of covering sin so that it no longer has the power of disturbing the covenant relation between God and man.[23]

When we take a wide-angle look at the Old Testament we see a tension between what might be called priestly religion and prophetic religion regarding sacrifice. Superficially, it appears that the classical prophets look negatively on the whole sacrificial system. There are indictments suggesting that God is nauseated with the offerings (Isa 1:11; Hos 8:11–13; Amos 5:21–23). Jeremiah even goes so far as to apparently deny that they were ordained by God: "Thus says the Lord of hosts, the God of Israel: Add your burnt offerings to your sacrifices, and eat the flesh. For in the day that I brought your ancestors out of the land of Egypt, I did not speak to them or command them concerning burnt offerings and sacrifices" (Jer 7:21–22).

What is one to make of this? When these passages are placed in context it is readily apparent that while the sacrifices are being offered, those who offer them are continuing in violation of the covenant law. In fact, that point is unequivocal in Jeremiah who follows the words quoted above with these: "But this command I gave them, 'Obey my voice, and I will be your God, and you shall be my people; and walk only in the way that I command you, so that it may be well with you'" (v. 23).

Unless one is willing to simply reject the teaching of the Torah, which declares that the sacrifices were initiated by God himself, and say, as one Old Testament theologian did, that the sacrifices were man's expedient for his own salvation, we must come to some other conclusion. The conclusion, which seems to be logically entailed, is that Israel was offering their sacrifices to God as a propitiation so that he would be satisfied and they could continue their antinomian lifestyle with impunity.

---

crucial issue and on this basis concludes, "Propitiation in relation to the one true God is quite distinct from propitiation in relation to the supposed deities projected from man's warped imagination." Ibid. This is certainly true but the question he leaves unanswered is, what is the difference? That is in fact the rock on which the whole idea of propitiation makes shipwreck.

23. Culpepper, *Interpreting the Atonement*, 28; cf. also 23–30.

Therefore it is a feasible inference from the larger picture to say that the prophets were condemning the practice of sacrifices because they were being offered for the wrong reasons. Furthermore there were cases in the Old Testament where sins were forgiven without sacrifice (e.g. Ps 51:16–17 appears to be of this genre). Additionally, there were times when sacrifices were not possible such as during the Captivity and when Antiochus Epiphanes had defiled the temple. Was it not possible during these times to have an experience of divine forgiveness? The answer is certainly, "yes!"

An additional issue needs to be addressed regarding the sins covered (not hidden) by the relevant offerings. Although it is explicitly stated that they are restricted to inadvertent sins, some of the sins that are listed exceed the definition of *inadvertent* or cultic. They can only be willful. Jewish scholar Jacob Milgrom, has offered a compelling explanation of this anomaly in what he calls the *priestly doctrine of repentance*. If these sins are repented of they may be reduced to the level of inadvertent sins and therefore may be expiated by sacrifice.[24]

There are further issues that arise out of the actual rituals themselves but since they more directly impinge on matters we shall discuss later, we defer comments on them until the more appropriate setting.

The Meaning of Sin

The discussions thus far have occasionally raised the matter of the meaning of "sin." Since a systematic explanation of the work of Christ must include a consistent understanding of the sickness that is addressed by God's redemptive action, we must explore the Biblical understanding.

First and foremost we must recognize that sin is a religious concept because, biblically, it has to do with mankind's relation to God. As Norman Snaith states it: "The word 'sin' can be used either in an ethical sense of transgressing a moral code, or as a religious term in the sense of rebellion against God, and so being alien to Him." But the prophetic use of the term, he demonstrates, is not ethical but religious since for them religion is "primarily a matter of relationship with God, and secondarily is a matter of ethics."[25]

While it may not be possible to capture the range of meanings implicit in the biblical concept of sin in terms of one formula, it may not

---

24. Milgrom, "Sacrifice."
25. Snaith, *Distinctive Ideas*, 60–61.

be amiss to suggest that its essence may be best understood in terms of alienation or estrangement.[26]

This alienation takes two different forms. The first form is the result of *rebellion*. The second is mankind's alienation from their created destiny, a destiny embodied in the concept of the *imago dei*. Thus to provide an adequate remedy for the human predicament, both forms must be addressed. The former in reconciliation and the latter in sanctification understood as the renewal of human persons in the image of God.

Most of the biblical material dealing with sin in the Old Testament takes place within a covenant context. It fact, it may be said that it is exclusively a covenant term. This does not imply that only God's people can sin, it rather broadens the concept of covenant. The one place where this becomes explicit is in Amos' prophetic oracles of judgment upon those pagan nations surrounding Israel (Amos 1:2—2:5). These nations come under the judgment of God because of cruelty to other human beings, which violates what Amos calls in 1:9 a "covenant of brotherhood" (NKJV) or "kinship."

Within the covenant relation established at Horeb, sin takes the form of disobedience to the covenant code and the basic word for sin (*pesha'*) means "rebellion," suggesting a willful behavior. All the classical prophets (Amos, Hosea, Isaiah and Micah) think of sin as fundamentally a rebellion against God. As previously noted, the English rendering of the key term as "transgression" is misleading because it gives the impression that the prophets are thinking of sin as primarily a transgression of a law.[27]

The same implication is found in 1 John 3:4, which probably comes nearest to being a connotative definition of sin of any New Testament passage. Once again, the confusion of ethics with religion has led the Authorized Version to translate it as "sin is the transgression of the law." Most modern versions accurately render it: "sin is lawlessness." This is tantamount to rebellion, an attitude of declaring one's independence from authority, in this case the Father.

Such sins, willful in nature, high handed in character, must be forgiven in response to repentance. And if what we have heretofore argued

---

26. F. W. Dillistone notes that "If Paul Tillich is in any way right in his assertions that 'the Christian message provides the answers to the questions implied in human existence'; . . . then everything points to the fact that it is precisely the doctrine of the Atonement which is needed to answer the most pressing enquiries of our own time . . . For in whatever direction we look . . . one question overshadows all others. It is the question of Alienation or Estrangement" (*The Christian Understanding of the Atonement*, 2).

27. Snaith, *Distinctive Ideas*, 63–64.

has any merit, God, like the father of the prodigal son, waits at the gate with no problem in embracing the repentant son (dirty rags, pig slop and all) who "comes to himself," abandons his rebellion and returns home.

The dominant use of "sin" (*harmartia*) in the New Testament appears to be in relation to the second form of alienation. Paul's sustained indictment of humanity, both Jew and Gentile, in Romans culminates with his empirically demonstrated conclusion: "For all have sinned and come short of the glory of God"(3:23). But here, as in other places (e.g. 2 Cor 3:18) in the New Testament, the term "glory" is a synonym for "image."

Without extensive elaboration, we simply want to point out here that the *imago dei* is now widely understood as a relational concept[28] and such an understanding entails a personal element. Thus, if sin is rebellion against God, a restoration of relationship through reconciliation is of necessity personal in nature and therefore the full benefits of the atonement should most appropriately be seen in a personal-relational paradigm.

One other piece of the puzzle needs to be put in place in order to round out the full picture. The central claim of the satisfaction theories may fairly be said to interpret the death of Christ as a sacrifice that propitiates the wrath of God. This suggests that this theme needs to be biblically understood.

Even those who make the idea of propitiated wrath a centerpiece of their doctrine of the atonement insist that God's wrath is to be differentiated from the emotional and capricious anger characteristic of pagan deities. Connell, who makes a strong argument for propitiation, rejects the interpretation of C. H. Dodd that "Paul retains the concept of the 'wrath of God' not to describe the attitude of God to man, but to describe the inevitable process of cause and effect in a moral universe," but approves the statement of Vincent Taylor that "by wrath Paul means not passionate irrational anger, but the judgment which falls upon sin in the moral world over which God rules."[29]

However, he nowhere explains how these views are essentially different. In fact they are not.

At the heart of this issue is whether or not the wrath of God should be interpreted as *personal* or *impersonal*.[30] Dodd is perhaps the most prominent proponent of the impersonal view. In his commentary on Romans, he finds that Paul never uses the verb "to be angry" with God as subject.

---

28. I have explored this in some detail as a basis for a Christian ethic in *Reflecting the Divine Image*.

29. Connell, "The Propitiatory Element in the Atonement."

30. Cf. Taylor, "Wrath."

The language is uniformly "the wrath of God," not "God's wrath." From this evidence he concludes that "wrath is not to be understood as a feeling or attitude of God toward us (as love and mercy should properly be) but rather as some process or effect of human sin; mercy is not the effect of human goodness but is inherent in the character of God." In a word, wrath is impersonal as we noted above.[31]

George Eldon Ladd generally agrees with Dodd but demurs on the idea that it is impersonal: "The New Testament concept of the wrath of God is not to be understood as equivalent to the anger of pagan deities, which could be turned to good will by suitable offerings . . . In Paul, the wrath of God is not an emotion telling how God feels, it tells us rather how he acts toward sin—and sinners.[32]

V. Taylor, C. H. Dodd and G. E. Ladd all concur that the wrath of God is the judgment that occurs as the consequence of this being a moral universe. It is unclear how the positions are really distinct from each other unless those who argue for the personal view see wrath as a feeling expressing various degrees of emotional animosity, but this is precisely what is rejected. Apparently the two can only be distinguished by whether or not we say God is directly active in each case of judgment or whether judgments should be interpreted in a "deistic" manner. If one can accept Paul Tillich's understanding of God as the "Ground of Being" or "Being Itself" with its implications for the God-world relation, this distinction will disappear.

But if the "wrath of God" is as sharply distinguished from the wrath of pagan deities as every Christian theologian seems to do, then the conclusion of Whiteley is unavoidable:

> . . . if the notion of the wrath of God has been so transformed, the notion of propitiation must be transformed *pari passu*. The recoil of God against sin must not be quenched, or God will cease to be Holy. God's hatred of sin can be "propitiated" only by the abolition of sin, Christ deals with sin, not by throwing a cloth over the eyes of God but by setting us, at the cost of his own life, in a relationship within which sin can be done away.[33]

The final resolution of the meaning of the wrath of God should result from a careful analysis of the use of the concept in scripture. This task

---

31. Dodd, *The Epistle of Paul to the Romans*, 47–50.

32. Ladd, *Theology of the New Testament*, 407. See Whiteley, *The Theology of St. Paul*, 61–72 for an extensive exegetical justification of this position.

33. Whiteley, *The Theology of Paul*, 147.

cannot be adequately pursued by word studies alone but by the attempt to view the use of the language contextually.

There are 17 different Hebrew words for various nuances of the word "wrath" used in the Old Testament. The New Testament employs 6 Greek words. Overall, taken together there is a total of 189 references in the Old and 50 in the New.[34]

There are two considerations for understanding the theme of wrath in the Old Testament: 1) the attribution of everything that occurs, both good and evil, to God. The modern Christian who is exposed to the Old Testament for the first time is in for a real culture shock. The Old Testament takes its monotheism seriously and is not squeamish about crediting evil to Yahweh.[35] 2) The second is a liberal use of anthropopathic symbolism. In ascribing human emotions to God, language that suggests, among other things, the "flaring of the nostrils" as reflecting the "hot" anger of God is used.

A further consideration that needs to be taken into account is how God's wrath is identified or recognized. Since God is known by what he does—his mighty acts—in redemptive behavior, the same principle must apply to his acts of judgment (wrath). The extent to which human knowledge has access to the divine being, as illustrated by the encounter between Moses and Yahweh in Exodus 33:18–23, eliminates the possibility of humans knowing *how God feels* in distinction from *what he does*.

With this stipulation, we must observe that both God's redemptive acts and his judgmental acts are identified as such through eyes of faith. Only the most naïve concept of objective knowledge will argue that God's action in history is unequivocally self-evident. All historical events are subject to diverse interpretations. Thus, as we shall see in a subsequent analysis of the biblical references, events in history that are objective in nature are interpreted by the Biblical writer as the wrath of God being manifested.

Analysis of the numerous uses of the Hebrew words that may be translated as "wrath" reveals that they fall into several different categories. Thirty Seven references refer to human anger and may thus be excluded from consideration. By far, the majority of texts (50) have to do with God's wrath at the disobedience of his covenant people. The question is, how is this to be identified? In the most explicit cases, God's wrath takes the

---

34. Based on *Young's Analytical Concordance*.

35. An interesting exception is 1 Chronicles 21:1 where David's census is reported as being inspired by Satan. The earlier account in 2 Samuel 24 attributes the census to God's initiative. Chronicles is late, doubtless after the encounter with other cultures had created a sense of dualism in Israel.

form of military disaster. In 2 Chronicles 12:12, the wrath of judgment is turned away by repentance. In Isaiah 10:6, Assyria is specifically named as the agent of God's anger. In cases of individuals, sickness, financial loss, or similar matters are viewed as God's wrath. This is especially present, as one would expect, in the book of Job. Job sees his own anguish as an expression of God's wrath upon him, yet God is not angry at Job but at Job's friends for falsely equating suffering with sin.

There does not seem to be a single instance in the Old Testament where the use of the wrath of God conforms to the interpretation placed upon it by those who advocate the satisfaction theory of the atonement. Rather, the wrath of God related to rebellion or sin is, or may be, usually averted by repentance and change of life. We have yet to examine the New Testament use of the concept.[36]

One of the most fruitful approaches to an understanding of many central truths of scripture is to explore the theological implications of the early Genesis narratives. Usually the specific terms are absent. After all, the Bible is neither a theological dictionary nor textbook. Formal theological propositions must be extrapolated from the personalistic language of scripture that is expressed in early Genesis in anthropomorphic images.

There are three images that are pertinent to the question under consideration here. The first is an implication from the decision to eat the forbidden fruit and the other two reflect the consequences of this act of disobedience. The temptation by the serpent included the suggestion that having eaten from the off-limits tree, the human pair would become like God. The Lord God concurred with this outcome, declaring "the man has become like one of us" (Gen 3:22). Did this mean that humanity had become divine in some sense? Logically it must have another significance. The most illuminating interpretation for this writer is that, while living in communion with the Creator, he chose what was good for the first pair. His concern was for their continued good and his wisdom was infallible.

---

36. The incident that might be an exception to this and has been used to support the idea of atonement by satisfaction to God is the incident recorded in Numbers 25 where Phinehas thrust a javelin through a Hebrew man and a Midianite woman engaged in intercourse with the result that Yahweh said to Moses: "Phinehas son of Eleazar, son of Aaron the priest, has turned back my wrath from the Israelites by manifesting such zeal among them on my behalf that in my jealousy I did not consume the Israelites" (v. 11, NRSV). But it is clearly stated that the "wrath" was manifested by a plague, which ceased when the situation was changed and punctuated by this dramatic, and violent action. At best we are left to considerable speculation concerning the precise details of this incident, which is clearly a theological interpretation. It would be extremely odd to derive a theological rationale for the death of Jesus from this incident.

Having grasped that prerogative from the all-wise Creator, it was assumed by Adam and Eve that they, not him, knew what was best for themselves. This result, coupled with their being alienated from the tree of life that was the source of their existence, was a disastrous situation in which all creation was in a counterflow against them. The words of Judges 5:20 picture life in which one sets himself against the created purpose of the universe: "the stars fought from heaven . . . against Sisera."

The second picture occurs at the time of worship, the tryst between the Creator and his highest creation. The act of disobedience had occurred and the Lord God in apparent ignorance of what had happened came to the garden sanctuary *as if* nothing had happened. On the surface this seems like a piece of naïve anthropomorphism but in reality it is a wonderful picture of the unconditional grace of God. The Creator did not remain at arm's length awaiting some movement on Adam's part to atone for his disobedience. There is no indication of his being angry or upset. Is this the result of ignorance on his part? I think not. This is a profoundly theological picture of God.

The corollary to this image is the pair cringing in the bushes, fearful of him who had been their Creator, their benefactor and the source of the meaningfulness that had characterized their garden existence, an existence best described as a state of *Shalom*.[37]

Their experience of God *now* is radically different from the day before. What made the difference? Had God changed? No! The change had resulted in an act that alienated them in their consciences as well as in reality from the Lord God. In that state of alienation they experienced the coming of the Creator to the trysting place as fear and anxiety that painted a completely different face on God. He was now a God of wrath due, not to his attitude toward them but to their new situation. Love and grace was experienced as judgment and wrath.

Has this situation changed with the dawning of the gospel age? Does the New Testament present a different picture? We will need to look at the relevant texts in context to ascertain if this is the case.

The uses of the two primary Greek terms (*thumos* and *orgē*) are more difficult to classify than the Hebrew. However, when the large number of references to human and demonic wrath are eliminated, the majority of

---

37. Elmer Martens describes the pre-Fall state beautifully as the embodiment of *shalom*: "But in Eden, as the opening chapters of Genesis describe it, that wholeness exists. Man is in tune with God, Adam and Eve are unashamed with each other; they live in harmony with themselves as well as with animals. Not only their needs but their desires are fully met. Here is the perfect state" (*God's Design*, 28).

references to the wrath of God are eschatological, a reflection of the day of the Lord theme of the Old Testament. And as James S. Stewart says in an analysis of the concept, "what we are concerned with is God's existing relation to men. Passages plainly eschatological are therefore not relevant here." Excluding these, references to the wrath of God are few and far between. Stewart further notes, soundly, that "What Paul means by the wrath of God—in its present, non-eschatological sense—is the totality of the divine reaction to sin."[38]

The implication of this way of understanding the wrath of God impinges on the issue of reconciliation. It would seem that Paul's unequivocal statement in 2 Corinthians 5:19 would put the matter beyond dispute. However the legal mentality of the West has, as we have seen, regularly argued that God must be reconciled by some propitiatory sacrifice.[39]

No doubt it is correct to say that when the estrangement between man and God is overcome, something happens on both sides of the relation. At least Jesus says in Luke 15:10, ". . . There is joy in the presence of the angels of God over one sinner who repents." But James S. Stewart is on target when he says,

> Surely what happens on God's side is so essentially different from what happens on man's side that to apply the one term to both can only cause confusion. Far wiser is it to follow the explicit guidance of the New Testament, which recognized the danger and was careful to avoid it. Where reconciling has to be done, God is always the subject, never the object. This is Christianity's distinctive glory. And "be ye reconciled to God" is its challenge.[40]

---

38. Stewart, *A Man in Christ*, 218–19.

39. In a very curious case of special pleading, the late Richard S. Taylor argued that "The phrase 'reconciling the world unto himself' does not mean what at first blush it seems to mean." In a word, Paul said exactly the opposite of what he meant. *God's Integrity and the Cross*, 30. This is even stranger in the light of the fact that Taylor published a book some years before arguing for a "verbal inerrancy" theory of Biblical inspiration. On the same text Albert Outler comments that "in the forensic model of justification, the meaning of 1 Corinthians [sic, should be 2 Cor] 5:19 had been reversed, as if St. Paul had said that 'God was in Christ reconciling himself to the world . . .'" (*Theology in the Wesleyan Spirit*, 53).

40. Stewart, *A Man in Christ*, 222.

9

The Rythmn of Redemption

All the preceding analyses suggest a three-fold movement in the redemptive work of Christ as it impinges on personal experience: identification—representation—identification. His identification with us is the basis for his representation of us, to which we respond by identifying with him. All of these have appeared (often seriatim) in the preceding expositions. We turn now to a fuller elaboration of this rhythm.

Identification

The incarnation itself is the central act of identification in that by this act of condescension, God in the person of his Son became flesh and tabernacled among us (John 1:14). The patristic debates concerning the person of Christ rejected several proposed rational explanations of the incarnation that failed to provide for the full identification of him who was fully God with the human situation. While the resultant creeds never removed the mystery, they clearly affirmed the full humanity of Jesus Christ. They affirmed that the Logos was *homoousios* (of one substance) with the Father and in the incarnation, became *homoousios* with humankind.

The question still remains concerning the significance of this assumption of human nature, particularly the extent of that identification. Traditionally, at least in the West, it was assumed and taught that the flesh assumed by the Logos was that of human nature as it was prior to the fall.[1]

The most recognizable voice dissenting from this position was Edward Irving who, on the basis of his claim that the Logos assumed fallen human nature and other deviations from accepted orthodoxy, was judged a heretic by the Church of Scotland. There were several little

---

1. H. Orton Wiley says of the virgin birth, ". . . the child was conceived with all the essential properties of original humanity, the accidental quality of sin in the fallen Adamic race excluded." *Christian Theology*, 2:148.

known proponents of the same position prior to Irving, the best known being Gregory of Nyssa.

However since Karl Barth advocated this position, there have been several reputable scholars who have accepted that view. It needs to be said that all of the advocates of this position, with one possible exception, affirm the sinlessness of Jesus. This is not the point at issue. It is the nature of the humanity that is assumed that is in question.[2]

According to Colin Gunton, Irving defends his position that "at the incarnation the Son did not assume the perfect, unfallen, flesh of Adam, but our fallen human nature" by two groups of arguments: The first group is ontological in nature. "If Jesus is born in human history to a human mother, then his body necessarily consists of matter that partakes of the fallenness of the world." The second group is soteriological in nature and directly relates to the Cappidocian argument that what is unassumed is unhealed. "In order to redeem the human will from bondage," Irving wrote, "the Son must take up into Himself the very conditions of a human will."[3]

One major difficulty in coming to terms with this claim is identifying precisely what is meant by "fallen human nature." Harry Johnson defines it simply as "human nature that is open to the possibility of sin." But unless more than this is said, nothing significant is said since the Genesis picture of unfallen humanity obviously allowed this possibility. Hence Johnson more carefully nuances his definition: "It is a nature that has been affected by the Fall, and by the sin and rebellion of previous generations."[4] This still remains somewhat vague.

The discussion of this issue soon leads to the question of the meaning of original sin, which is one of the reasons, if not the principal one, for the traditional rejection of this view of the identification of the Son with humanity.

If, with one form of the Augustinian tradition, we hold that the essence of sin is concupiscence, which is dominantly manifested in sexuality, and sin is propagated by the act of conception this would seem to offer a strong argument against Irving's contention. It is this assumption, however, that led to the interpretation of the virgin birth as the divine ploy to avoid

---

2. Cf. Johnson, *The Humanity of the Savior*, 129–50. Johnson lists among those supporting this view J. A. T. Robinson, T. F. Torrance, Nels F. S. Ferré, C. E. B. Cranfield, Harold Roberts, Lesslie Newbigin, and Colin Gunton who has been vocal in advocating Irving's Christology.

3. Quoted in Gunton, "Two Dogmas Revisited: Edward Irving's Christology," 359–76.

4. Johnson, *The Humanity of the Saviour*, 22, 24.

the contamination of transmitted corruption. But this is an indictment of the biblical understanding of creation. Furthermore, it would seem to require that one posit a near infinite regress of immaculate conceptions to avoid the corruption of original sin unless we are prepared to affirm this of Jesus. Original sin is not restricted to the male gender.

If original sin is interpreted to mean original guilt so that we are guilty of Adam's actual sin, no matter how our relation to Adam is conceived, then we are faced with a difficult decision since it certainly seems contradictory to speak of Jesus as guilty. Of course, neither of these two interpretations is acceptable.

If, however, we follow a different line of interpretation that sees original sin to basically be a deprivation of the Holy Spirit that results in depravation, it seems altogether possible to accept this position. Jesus' conception by the Holy Spirit and Luke's emphasis on Jesus' return from his victory over the tempter in the wilderness "filled with the power of the Spirit" (Luke 4:14) might lend credence to the view that his unbroken obedience to the Father entailed the unbroken enabling presence of the Spirit. To take this line of thought would require one to distinguish Jesus' filling from that of John the Baptist, and also demonstrate the difference between this filling from birth and the baptism bestowment. While viewing original sin in this way may make possible the reading that Jesus assumed fallen human nature, it definitely does not make it a necessary conclusion.

Many today deny the historicity of a state of integrity prior to a fall and therefore, as Paul Tillich taught, simply living under the conditions of existence places one in a state of alienation from her essence. That is to say, creation and fall are virtually synonymous. According to such a view, the incarnation would entail fallen human nature.

Colin Gunton offers his own rationale for this position that avoids the problems of traditional views of original sin and does not necessarily deny the historicity of the fall. It builds upon the concept of solidarity that is indigenous to biblical modes of thought about humanness: "To be a human creature is to be constituted, to be made what one is, by and in a network of relations. So far as one's being is concerned these relations are two fold, horizontal and vertical. The uniqueness of Jesus is that He alone is constituted by the intersection of these two relations." In fact, Gunton argues that "one chief function of the doctrine of the virgin birth is accordingly to say something about Jesus' humanity, and thus to place him in a particular way at the intersection of the horizontal and vertical dimensions."[5]

Concerning the horizontal relatedness, "when we say of Jesus that he is of one substance with ourselves, sin apart, part of what we mean is that like us, he was a particular human being, a determinate person, made what he was in part by his genes and the history and society of the world in which he came to be."[6]

The implication of this is that unless Jesus was other than we are—not *homoousios* with us—he is inevitably involved in the structures of a disordered race, in a situation of alienation from God. Harry Johnson seems to be making the same assumption as he explores the option that Jesus assumed fallen human nature. He says, "It must be underlined . . . that in the definition of 'fallen human nature' that has been given, the alienation involved in the assumption of this nature was in no way personal. Personal alienation only arises when personal sin and rebellion enter into the situation and guilt is incurred."[7]

All this is suggesting that fallen human nature simply means involvement in what moderns call systemic evil from which none are exempt. This view is, of course, in strong tension with an individualistic view of human personhood. But the relational understanding of personhood is now rather generally acknowledged.[8]

This whole issue impinges on the question of the impeccability of Christ. Was it, or was it not possible for Him to sin? One of the major differences between the Alexandrian and the Antiochian Christologies related to this question. With their concern for morality, the Antiochians insisted on the reality of Jesus' temptations whereas the Alexandrians, with their soteriological interests, tended to affirm that sinning was an ontological impossibility.[9]

In a survey of the New Testament evidence, Harry Johnson is able to show that numerous passages, including certain episodes in Jesus' life such as his baptism, do allow for the possible interpretation that he assumed fallen human nature, but none of them establish the necessity of it. Therefore it remains a hypothesis which, if true, involves the most com-

---

5. Gunton, *Christ and Creation*, 36, 52.
6. Ibid., 41.
7. Johnson, *The Humanity of the Saviour*, 33.
8. For an excellent elaboration of this understanding see Anderson, *On Being Human*.
9. See Kelly, *Early Christian Doctrines*, 280ff.

plete identification with the human situation possible, "yet without sin" (Heb 4:15).

The event that marks Jesus most intimate identification with the human situation was in his death. In the light of the Pauline teaching that the universal evidence of fallenness is death (Rom 5), death is the most poignant symbol not only of our finitude and mortality but of our fallenness as well. The most difficult aspect of this truth emerges out of the cry of dereliction from the cross. How is this to be explained? According to the penal satisfaction theory of the atonement, it is fairly easy to explain: Jesus was really abandoned by the Father as he was made a substitute for the sinner and bore the wrath of God. But this creates severe problems regarding the involvement of God in the redemptive process and raises questions regarding the trinity.

Our theological sensibilities resonate with F. W. Dillistone when he says: "Whatever his suffering means, it does not mean that God has abandoned him or even temporarily turned away from him. Never is the Son nearer to the Father's heart than in the hour of his bitterest trial; never is the Father nearer to the Son than in the moment of his deepest identification with those he had come to save."[10]

John McLeod Campbell, among others, believed that when Jesus uttered these words found at the beginning of Psalm 22, he was thinking about the entire Psalm, which is an expression of trust in God that concludes with a cry of victory. This interesting interpretation does not seem to have gained much support, however.

Vincent Taylor sees the words as an existential cry of despair growing out of Jesus' full identification with the human situation:

> The saying expresses a feeling of utter desolation, a sense of abandonment by the Father, an experience of defeat and despair . . . The suffering is not punishment directly inflicted by God, and is penal insofar as it is sharing in the sense of desolation and loss which sin brings in its train when it is seen and felt for what it is . . . Jesus so closely identifies Himself with sinners, and experienced the horror of sin to such a degree, that for a time His communion with the Father was broken, so that His face was obscured and He seemed to be forsaken by Him.[11]

---

10. Dillistone, *Jesus Christ and His Cross*, 27–28.

11. Taylor, *Jesus and His Sacrifice*, 161. This quotation is cited with strong approval by Moody, *Word of Truth*, 372.

This perspective is not a recent liberal view as is seen by Thomas Oden's citations of words to this effect by two of the early church fathers. Leo says it is not "as if, when Jesus was fixed upon the wood of the cross, the Omnipotence of the Father's Deity had gone away from Him; seeing that God's and Man's Nature were so completely joined in Him that the union could not be destroyed by punishment nor by death." Gregory of Nazianzen wrote, "It was not he who was forsaken either by the Father or by his own Godhead but, as I said, he was in his own person representing us. For we were the forsaken and despised before but now by his representative act saved."[12]

Is such an identification really possible? James R. Newby tells about Quaker John Woolman who experienced a vision in which he was so "mixed with" the suffering people he saw that "henceforth he could no longer consider himself a distinct or separate being. Their suffering was his suffering . . . They were connected."[13] If a mere mortal could experience this depth of identification, it is surely possible for the God-man.

Harry Johnson, in seeking to defend the incarnation as the assumption of fallen human nature, argues that this cry of dereliction indicates how full was the identification of Jesus with the human condition and suggests that "if Jesus stands outside the company of fallen mankind we must accept either the doctrine of substitution or leave the link with sinful humanity unexplained; there seems no escape from this dilemma." In the light of his hypothesis he offers the insightful observation that "on the Cross, there took place the decisive battle between Jesus and the powers of evil, not simply powers that were external, but also the power of the 'fallen nature' that He had inherited. Here on the Cross there was the purging of human nature." He believes this makes the unity of the incarnation and the atonement a reality,[14] a point we have been seeking to defend. His identification with us becomes the basis of his representative function.

Representation

One thing needs to be said prior to the exploration of this topic. Of necessity it will be incomplete, even one-sided, since unlike the implication of

---

12. Oden, *The Word of Truth*, 333. Note the Christological basis of these judgments, a principle that Oden apparently abandons in relation to the issue of "passibility" quoting approvingly several fathers who say that Christ is passible (able to suffer) according to his human nature, impassible (incapable of suffering) with respect to the divine nature. This clearly reflects the Nestorian heresy. See our previous discussion of this issue.

13. Quarterly newsletter from Yokefellows, Int., n.d.

14. Johnson, *The Humanity of the Saviour*, 62–63.

satisfaction views, representation entails both a subjective and an objective side. To see the full significance of this theme, we will have to await the next section on identification. Otherwise it will be like the "sound of one hand clapping," an unimaginable thought to a non-Buddhist.

The theme of representation is solidly grounded in the biblical concept of corporate personality. Covenants are often established with a representative figure who is understood to embody the group in his own person. When God covenants with Abraham it is in principle the establishing of a relationship with all Abraham's descendents who respond to the promise. This does not mean that inclusion in the covenant was automatic but each generation (even individuals) had to renew the covenant although it was not a new covenant but incorporation into the original one. The Hebrew concept of corporate personality gave validity to this relation and enabled the heirs of the covenant to consider themselves as really being present in the person of their representative when the covenant was originally instituted. This explains the use of the plural pronouns in Hebrew confessions of faith such as Deuteronomy 5:2–3: "The Lord our God made a covenant with us in Horeb. Not with our ancestors [alone] did the Lord make this covenant, but with us, who are all of us here alive today."

Another symbolic manifestation of the representative function is the breastplate of the high priest. As he enters the Holy of Holies on the Day of Atonement, the names of the 12 tribes are inscribed on his chest signaling that he stands before God on their behalf.

Not quite so unambiguous are the ritual sacrifices that function to maintain the covenant relation (see above). When the offerer brings his animal to be sacrificed, he lays his hands on the head of the victim. It is easy to infer that the animal is to perish as a substitute for the one who has become unclean, so he will not perish. But the fact that the offering is still regarded as holy militates against this interpretation. More likely, the sacrifice functions as the representative of the one who makes the offering. The interpretation of H. H. Rowley resonates with this function and more nearly with the whole tenor of scripture:

> The sacrificial animal was not merely a substitute for the offerer. He laid his hands upon it and was conceived of as in some way identified with it, so that in its death he was conceived of as dying—not physically, but spiritually. The death of the victim symbolized his death to his sin, or to whatever stood between him and God, or his surrender of himself to God in thankfulness and humility.[15]

---

15. Rowley, *The Meaning of Sacrifice in the Old Testament*, 88.

One very important semantic consideration needs to be noted here. When the New Testament emphasizes that the work of Christ is *for us*, it carries a special connotation. There are two Greek words that may be translated "for." One is *Anti*, which suggests the notion of substitution and means "instead of." The other is *huper*, which implies "on behalf of." It is the latter term that is predominantly used by St. Paul thus his emphasis is on what Christ did for us by his representation "on our behalf." Vincent Taylor argues that the meaning of the death of Christ as vicarious in Paul's understanding is in his phrase "for us." He points out that in all cases except one he uses the preposition *huper* meaning "on behalf of." In 1 Thessalonians 5:10 (the one exception) he uses *peri*, "on account of," which, Taylor insists, is not appreciably different from *huper*. Nowhere does he use *anti*, "instead of." From this, he concludes, we may certainly infer that he did not look upon the death of Christ as that of a substitute. The alleged substitutionary element in his thought is rather to be discerned in his teaching about the representative work of Christ.

In our proposed taxonomy of atonement theories in chapter 1 we identified four representative views. The ransom theory is probably a bit loosely correlated with this view but as the ransom price paid to the captor (Satan) the Son did not serve as a substitute but as the representative one.

In John McLeod Campbell's alternative to the legal paradigm that characterized the penal theory, he taught a view of vicarious penitence whereby Christ offered a perfect repentance on behalf of sinful man. This has had its detractors as well as its defenders (see below) but the point here is that Christ functions as our representative.

In Aulén's reconstruction of the dramatic theory, Jesus clearly serves as our representative as he fights on our behalf the powers of evil and overcomes them. His victory that occurred throughout his ministry, consummated by the cross/resurrection/ascension may now be ours by identification with him by faith.

The contemporary scholar who is perhaps the most explicit defender of the representative view of the work of Christ is the Methodist New Testament scholar, Vincent Taylor. His thesis includes two very important considerations:

1) While modern theology generally identifies forgiveness and reconciliation (and identifies justification as Paul's version of forgiveness), he argues that the New Testament does not do so but teaches that justification is not merely a Pauline equivalent for forgiveness but is a distinctive moment in the story of God's dealing with mankind, and that

while forgiveness, justification and reconciliation form an indissoluble unity, they must be distinguished. Forgiveness is the prerequisite for reconciliation, and justification is the gracious act of God that makes reconciliation ethically possible. This is consistent with the analysis of justification presented earlier.

2) No theory of the atonement is adequate that does not provide for *all* the benefits identified in the New Testament: forgiveness, justification, reconciliation, fellowship with God and sanctification.

These benefits are provided, he insists, by seeing the work of Christ as representative. Borrowing a phrase from John Wesley, he recognizes that this interpretation is but "a hair's breadth" from the substitutionary theory. As noted above, he believes that the sacrificial imagery provides the most significant clue to the representative model. But he argues that "in claiming that the work of Christ is sacrificial we are far removed from the propitiatory ideas that are sub-Christian in their character and implications."[16]

The major problem with this way of interpreting the atonement is the limited use of the imagery of sacrifice in the New Testament. Taylor admits this limitation but argues that he is justified in taking it beyond the letter of the New Testament teaching because of its adequacy in interpreting the atonement. He says

> The sacrificial category is peculiarly suitable for this doctrinal presentation because, in the use of the term "blood," it suggests the thought of life, dedicated, offered, transformed, and open to our spiritual appropriation, and because in its basal suggestion of an offering which the worshipper may make his own, it supplies a religious pattern for the needs of thought, devotional culture, worship, and service.[17]

By living a life of perfect obedience to the Father, including being "obedient to the point of death—even death on a cross" (Phil 2:8) the Son can offer to God a sacrifice that is fully acceptable to the holiness of God. He did this on our behalf so that we, by faith, can identify ourselves with him and experience full reconciliation to God. In Taylor's words: "The true view of the substitutionary activity of Jesus is one which recognizes that in his suffering and death he has expressed and effected that which no individual man has the power or spirituality to achieve, but into which,

16. Taylor, *Jesus and His Sacrifice*, 198.
17. Ibid.

in virtue of an ever-deepening fellowship with him, men can progressively enter so that it becomes their offering to God."[18]

This takes us logically to the third theme of this rhythm of redemption.

Identification

The representative function of Christ requires that its effectiveness depends upon our identification with Him. This is the "other hand" that completes the rhythm. We have already seen intimations of this in seeking to describe the representative phase of the atonement.

All the proposals we have explored, with the exception of certain versions of the penal substitutionary theory, emphasize the necessity of our existential participation in the atoning work of Christ. Campbell's teaching of a vicarious penitence by Christ is to be accepted by "'the Amen of our individual spirits,' it is not offered as a substitute for our own repentance."[19]

In an earlier discussion we noticed how R. C. Moberly developed a similar position as Campbell. But he qualifies his view of a "sacrifice of supreme penitence" in these words:

> We are now hundreds of miles from the thought of vicarious punishment . . . Even if, in a sense, we may consent to speak of vicarious penitence; yet it is not exactly vicarious. He indeed consummated penitence in Himself before the eyes, and before the hearts, of men who were not penitent themselves. But He did so, not in the sense that they were not to repent, or that His penitence was a substitute for theirs. He did so, not as a substitute, not even as a delegated representative, but as that inclusive total of true Humanity, of which they were potentially, and were to learn to become, a part. He consummated penitence, not that they might be excused from the need of repenting, but that they might learn, in Him, their own true possibility of penitence.[20]

But the most important question concerns the Biblical adequacy of this aspect of what we are calling the rhythm of redemption. Even in the

---

18. Taylor, *Jesus and His Sacrifice*, 283.
19. Campbell, *The Nature of the Atonement*, 340.
20. Moberly, *Atonement and Personality*, 283f. V. Taylor comments on the criticisms of both Campbell and Moberly that those who dismiss their views revealed that their knowledge of these men was "neither recent nor profound." *The Doctrine of the Atonement*, 200, note 1.

Gospels, we hear anticipations of this theme in Jesus' calls to discipleship. The context of the stipulations for discipleship is the experience of Jesus himself: loneliness, homelessness, suspicion, opposition, self-denial, cross bearing, and death. The experience of the Master is to be replicated by those who follow him if they, indeed, identify with him.

But with Paul, who provides us with the most replete analyses of the appropriation of the benefits of the atonement, we see the idea of identification becoming a central motif. As quoted earlier D. E. H. Whiteley insists that "if St. Paul can be said to hold a theory of the *modus operandi* [of the atonement], it is the 'participation' theory: his other sayings are to be regarded as statements of the fact of the atonement, expressed by means of the religious language of Judaism."[21] This motif is so central that some scholars have argued that it is the controlling theme of his theology.[22]

But this emphasis comes most specifically to expression in relation to certain critical events in the life of Christ: we are identified with him in his baptism, we are crucified with him, and we are risen with Him.[23]

In Romans 6:1–4 Paul says: "What then are we to say? Should we continue in sin in order that grace may abound? By no means! How can we who died to sin go on living in it? Do you not know that all of us who have been baptized into Christ Jesus were baptized into his death? Therefore we have been buried with him by baptism into death? . . . so that, just as Christ was raised from the dead by the glory of the Father, so we too might walk in newness of life."

It is a commonplace that Paul is attempting here to reject the illegitimate antinomian inference from his doctrine of grace. But the implications for how the Christ event is to be appropriated is of great importance. Here the believer's baptism is understood as his or her identification with Jesus' baptism. For the believer the ritual has both a retrospective and a prospective dimension and Paul is here laying emphasis on the latter.

Jesus' baptism was his ordination into the role of the Suffering Servant, the vision by which he reinterpreted the messianic mission. It was a proleptic event in which he assumed the path that would lead eventually to the cross. In a word, it was a declaration of intent to die. It is this aspect that Paul is emphasizing. When we are buried with him in baptism, we are thereby declaring our intent to put to death the old life and bring into being a new form of existence.

21. Whiteley, The Theology of *Paul*, 134.

22. For discussion of this see Ridderbos, *Paul: An Outline of His Theology*.

23. One of the most sustained treatments of this theme, referred to widely in scholarly literature, is Tannehill, *Dying and Rising with Christ*.

How does one do this? That seems to be the implication of the Pauline testimony in Romans 6:6—"We know that our old self was crucified with him so that the body of sin might be destroyed, and we might no longer be enslaved to sin." The ego-centered existence is to be replaced by a Christ-centered existence and this entails a death to ego-centricity.

The result of this "expulsive power of a new affection" (Thomas Chalmers) is doubtless what the apostle meant when he spoke of being risen with Christ whereby one is to "seek the things that are above, where Christ is, seated at the right hand of God" (Col 3:1). This exhortation is not a call to an irrelevant heavenly-mindedness but rather to derive one's values from the risen and ascended Christ who came to this status by way of being submissive unto death.

There is a certain ambiguity involved in Paul's thought since, as Herman Ridderbos says, "the unfolding of the redemptive significance of Christ's death and resurrection, the fundamental motif of Paul's gospel, is like a multi-colored spectrum."[24] There are those elements that focus on bringing about a reconciliation to God and those that emphasize the transformation that results in the new life in Christ, or sanctification. These are not neatly separated as they might be in a theological textbook.

The nature of experience is doubtless such that, except in most unusual situations, a person who becomes a follower of Christ only comes to the recognition of the full implications of discipleship over a period of time. The result of this dawning consciousness of the full implications of the provisions of the atonement would be reflected in the development of Christian experience by stages within a dynamic process. This fact lies behind the statement of F. J. Huegel that "A study of Christian biography reveals the fact that the great saints of the Church . . . have with few exceptions experienced what some have called 'a second work of grace.'"[25]

John Wesley's teaching about the relation of sanctification to the structure of Christian experience doubtless reflects this reality. For him, neither scripture nor experience present us with a static structure to be imposed upon human experience, but a normal pattern that may be derived from it.

It should be noticed that when this larger picture is taken into account, the atonement provides for both justification (reconciliation) and sanctification thus addressing a concern expressed in the introductory chapter of this study. One major question remains. It is one thing to describe an exalted state of grace, it is another to provide the dynamic

---

24. Ridderbos, *Paul*, 159.
25. Huegel, *Bone of His Bone*, 25.

that enables weak and fallen humanity to approximate that ideal. This has been universally recognized as the most serious weakness of an exemplarist theory of the work of Christ. Is this provision also to be found in the New Testament understanding of the incarnation and atonement? To that question we now turn in the final chapter.

10

The Holy Spirit and the Atonement

WHEN ONE reads the Old Testament with appropriate sensitivity, especially the Psalms, it is not possible to doubt that forgiveness and acceptance by God was a present reality. Popular interpreters have often said that the sacrifices of the cult all looked forward to the great sacrifice that would put an end to all sacrifices suggesting that their efficacy was dependent upon a future event. But there is not a shred of evidence in the Old Testament itself for this position.¹ It is only from the vantage point of the New Testament view of the sacrifice of Christ that those Old Testament sacrifices are seen as temporary or provisional or preparatory, and even incomplete (see especially Hebrews). That is a Christian vision but not a Hebrew vision.

In the light of this fact alone, we must not infer that forgiveness was not possible until the death of Christ propitiated the Father. Furthermore the fact that throughout his ministry Jesus freely forgave sins—and in doing so his opponents recognized that he was assuming the prerogatives of God—further substantiates this claim. In fact, as Hendry observes, it was his claim to possess this authority, rather than his proclamation of judgment, that brought him into collision with the official representatives of the Jewish religion. In commenting on Mark 2:1–12, he says, "It should be noted that the 'blasphemy' of Jesus in the eyes of the scribes did not consist in his assuming that God is free to forgive, for they too took this for granted; it was his assumption of the authority to exercise this divine prerogative."²

While Jesus rather frequently indicated that his mission was incomplete until its completion at the cross, He never suggested that his words of absolution were conditioned upon a subsequent event. They were present reality.

---

1. It is true that prophets like Jeremiah and Ezekiel recognized the inadequacy of the Old Covenant provisions, and anticipated a better covenant but this did not relate to the sacrifices.

2. Hendry, *The Gospel of the Incarnation*, 113.

In addition, we find that the emphasis of the *kerygma* of the early church is in a different direction. C. H. Dodd's classic analysis identifies six components of the preaching of the first disciples:

1) the age of fulfillment has dawned;
2) this has occurred through the ministry, death, and resurrection of Jesus;
3) Jesus has been exalted to God's right hand;
4) the Holy Spirit has been given;
5) the crucified one will return in glory; and
6) finally an appeal for repentance, the offer of forgiveness, and the gift of the Holy Spirit.[3] And the uniqueness of this last point is the correlation between forgiveness and the gift of the Spirit. In context, it furthermore seems clear that repentance carries its literal meaning of a change of mind about the crucified one (see elaboration at the end of this chapter).

The central thrust of this outline of the New Testament gospel is upon the agency of Jesus of Nazareth in bringing to consummation the hopes or expectations of the Old Testament. While the language is not explicitly used in the Old Testament, it is appropriate to speak of this hope as revolving around the hope for the present and immanent reality of the Kingdom of God.[4]

This hope is expressed in a diversity of images that should not be forced into an artificial unity. But as Bruce Baloian says:

> In these descriptions of the age to come the spirit of God has a large role. Amidst the variety of descriptions of the new age, essential features of the spirit's work can be identified. The spirit will have a central role in the appearance and work of the Messiah, in the restoration of Israel, in the transformation of the individual, in the outpouring of the spirit on all, and in the creation of a new order.[5]

The intimate connection between their belief that the Kingdom of God had become a present reality in the life and ministry of Jesus and their experience of the Holy Spirit meant, as George C. Lyons says, that "early

---

3. Dodd, *The Apostolic Preaching*.
4. Cf. Bright, *The Kingdom of God*.
5. Baloian, "The Spirit of God in the Old Testament," 23.

Christians found it impossible to separate pneumatology and eschatology from christology."[6]

There seems to be a dual movement in the Old Testament connecting the Spirit with a future age.[7] One has to do with the function of the Spirit as an endowment upon leaders who are involved in bringing in the kingdom and the other with moral transformation.

Charismatic Leadership

George Hendry makes the observation that the activity of those who are indwelt, or empowered, by the Spirit of the Lord in the Old Testament was designed to establish the kingdom.[8] It is obvious that the concept of the Kingdom of God under the old covenant had different parameters than it came to have under the new. It generally was viewed there as synonymous with the establishment of Israel as a nation and often took the form of oracles against foreign nations that stood in the way of this goal. Especially in case of certain leaders like Moses and Samuel there was a dominant spiritual emphasis that gave to national concerns a pronounced theological significance. But although seldom completely absent by the very nature of the case, the spiritual dimension often could only be dimly observed. Essentially, the leadership in early Israel was charismatic in nature. With the inauguration of a monarchy, the first two kings (Saul and David) were recognized by Israel only because they were charismatic, i.e. endowed with the spirit of Yahweh. Beginning with Solomon, this shifted to largely dynastic qualifications.

It is important to notice the nature of the Old Testament experiences of being seized by the spirit of the Lord. Briefly stated, they were generally episodic, temporary, and not essentially related to moral character (e.g. Samson). H. B. Swete describes the action of the Spirit as involving "gifts of bodily strength and physical courage, as well as mental and spiritual capacities. More particularly, it is regarded as the source of the gift of prophecy."[9]

The gift predicted by Joel (2:28–29) that anticipated a democratization of the Spirit is of this genre and relates to the restoration of Judah and Jerusalem (3:1). Ezekiel's dramatic vision of the valley of dry bones

---

6. Lyons, "The Spirit in the Gospels," 38.

7. See an excellent discussion of these two themes in Hill, *Greek Words and Hebrew Meanings*.

8. Hendry, *The Holy Spirit in Christian Theology*.

9. Sweet, *The Holy Spirit in the New Testament*, 2.

emphasized the same point. The reconstituted Israel after the exile is an impotent force apart from the energizing of the breath (Spirit) of God (Ezek 27:10).

It seems fair to assume that the charismatic endowment of John the Baptist is of this same kind of empowerment as he announced the imminent coming of the Kingdom of God. *What is revolutionary is the way in which Jesus carries out his ministry of bringing in the kingdom through the power of the Holy Spirit.*

As Lyons explains: "Luke . . . carefully distinguishes between the Baptist's prophetic election and endowment and Jesus' miraculous conception by the Holy Spirit. The same God was active in both men, but in different ways and toward different ends."[10] The role of the Spirit in the virgin birth, reminiscent of the Spirit's activity in creation, suggests that "the part played by the Holy Spirit in the birth narratives is thus seen to be the fulfillment of God's promised redemption in a new act of creation, comparable with that of Genesis 1."[11]

At Jesus baptism the Holy Spirit came upon him in all his fullness and power (Matt 3:16; Mark 1:10; Luke 3:22; John 1:32, 33). But it was precisely in this event that the whole concept of charismatic leadership empowered to inaugurate the rule of God was proleptically transformed. The voice from heaven, citing a composite word from the suffering servant songs (Isa 42:10) and the inauguration of the messianic king (Ps 2:7), defined the pattern that Jesus' mission was to embody.

It was the Spirit who drove him into the wilderness to test his resolve to follow this new understanding of how God's rule was to become immanent in the world. Each test was a Satanic attempt to divert him from this call. After his successful contest with the power of evil, Luke tells us that he returned to Galilee "filled with the power of the Spirit"(4:14).

According to Gunton, Edward Irving draws upon the way the Gospels relate Jesus' success to the power of the Spirit to support his belief that Jesus assumed fallen human nature. "To bear fallen human flesh is necessary if Jesus is to complete the work to which he was called. What is important soteriologically was that Jesus was enabled to resist temptation not by some immanent conditioning, but by virtue of his obedience to the guidance of the Spirit."[12]

---

10. Lyons, "The Spirit in the Gospels," 41.
11. C. K. Barrett, quoted in ibid., 45.
12. Gunton, *Christ and Creation*, 54.

When Jesus announced the beginning of his public ministry in Nazareth, he read from Isaiah 61:1–2—"The Spirit of the Lord is upon me, because he has anointed me to bring good news to the poor, He has sent me to proclaim release to the captives and recovery of sight to the blind, to let the oppressed go free, to proclaim the year of the Lord's favor" (Luke 4:18–19).

Jesus' redefinition of the nature of charismatic leadership in terms of the suffering servant became the understanding that eventually came to be seen in the New Testament as the normative concept of the power of the Holy Spirit. This new realization may not have occurred immediately, but only gradually as the embodiment of the Spirit in Jesus took hold of the minds and hearts of the early church. It came to its clearest expression with Paul where "we find a richer conception and deeper exploration of the nature of the Spirit, of its activity and of *its inherent connection with Jesus Christ.*"[13]

James S. Stewart's evaluation of Paul's contribution to the understanding of the experience of the Holy Spirit captures the significance of what is implicit in the Gospels:

> In the primitive Christian community there was a tendency at the first—perhaps natural under the circumstances—to revert to the cruder conceptions of the Spirit, and to trace his working mainly in such phenomena as speaking in tongues. It was Paul who saved the nascent faith from that dangerous retrogression. Not in any accidental and extraneous phenomena, he insisted, not in any spasmodic emotions or intermittent ecstasies were the real tokens of God's Spirit to be found; but in the quiet, steady, normal life of faith, in power that worked on moral levels, in the soul's secret inward assurance of its sonship of God, in love and joy and peace and patience and a character like that of Jesus.

This poignant comment needs qualification. It is accurate in its evaluation of Paul's view of the Spirit but seems to imply that this is in contrast with Luke's understanding as recorded in Acts. It is generally accurate to say that subsequent interpretations of Acts have often focused selectively on those inaugural manifestations such as tongues-speaking but Luke's account is clearly designed to subordinate the Spirit to Christ as in the Paraclete discourses reported in the Fourth Gospel. In a word, as Frederick Dale Bruner puts it, "The ministry of the Spirit is Christocentricity."

---

13. Heron, *The Holy Spirit*, 44. Emphasis added.

In an exegetical study of the baptism of the Holy Spirit in the book of Acts, Bruner argues that "the opening paragraph of Acts has set the standard terms by which the Holy Spirit in the remainder of the book is to be understood. This paragraph," he says, "is the lexicon of the Spirit in Acts." What this means he describes as follows:

> Luke wishes here in an impressive introductory manner to connect the work of Jesus with the ministry of the Spirit. What Jesus did or continues to do was and is "through the Holy Spirit." Luke does not wish for the Holy Spirit, who is to play such an important role in Acts, to be separated from the work of Jesus Christ as though the Holy Spirit could be understood to have a separate, independent, or even analogous work of his own. Luke's first sentence makes clear an intention of his entire book: the Spirit is not to be dissociated from Jesus. The Spirit *is* Jesus at work in continuation of his ministry.[14]

Peter identifies the events on that first Pentecost as the fulfillment of the prophecy of Joel who "like Luke, finds the *point* of the great eschatological Spirit-event not so much in the pouring out of the Spirit as such as in the universal promise of salvation *for which* the Spirit is poured out."[15]

D. Lyle Dabney argues from the exegetical implications of the phrase, "Justified by the Spirit" (1 Tim 3:16; cf. also Rom 4:25) that the life-giving power of the Spirit manifested in the resurrection of Christ results in our understanding of salvation in Christ taking on "new and different contours than had previously been the case." In particular it would "help us to speak of God's redemption of creation as having to do with the entire life, death, and resurrection of Jesus Christ," and also with "the entirety of human life and death."

Pertinent to our emphasis on the pervertive influence of the juridical perspective on the work of Christ, he argues that this understanding of the significance of the whole Christ was "fatefully marginalized by the dominant traditions arising in the thirteenth and sixteenth centuries [Scholastic and Reformation traditions] and has been reclaimed but tragically misconstrued by the traditions which have arisen in the modern period (Holiness, Pentecostal and Charismatic traditions).[16]

---

14. Bruner, *A Theology of the Holy Spirit*, 156, 159.

15. Ibid., 165,

16. Dabney, "Justified by the Spirit," 46–67. His critique of the modern views of Spirit-Baptism is accurate only if one identifies the "Holiness" movement with certain marginal phases of the American Holiness movement of the nineteenth century. It is off the mark with John Wesley's theology of the Spirit and the best scholarship of the holiness

Hope of Moral Transformation

The second movement to which we referred was a growing recognition of the failure of the Mosaic covenant at one crucial point. That movement reached its climax with Jeremiah and Ezekiel. The repeated failure of Israel to maintain moral integrity by living out the covenant stipulations had led the nation of Judah to the brink of total destruction. The northern kingdom had already been destroyed for virtually uninterrupted moral failure.

What perplexed Jeremiah the most deeply was the foolishness of Judah's unfaithfulness. His penetrating analyses of the stupidity of sin is found in chapter two where, employing graphic plays on words, he described the insanity of her behavior. His inspired conclusion is that the problem is with the heart. The old covenant did not explicitly make provision for inward transformation or sanctification. Thus, in prophetic utterance, he foresaw that God would establish a new covenant with better provisions: "The days are surely coming, says the Lord, when I will make a new covenant with the house of Israel and the house of Judah. It will not be like the covenant that I made with their ancestors when I took them by the hand to bring them out of the land of Egypt—a covenant that they broke, though I was their husband, says the Lord. But this is the covenant that I will make with the house of Israel after those days, says the Lord: I will put my law within them, and I will write it on their hearts; and I will be their God, and they shall be my people" (Jer 31:31–33).

Ezekiel describes the same hope in cultic language as one would expect from a priest: "I will sprinkle clean water upon you, and you shall be clean from all your uncleannesses, and from all your idols I will cleanse you. A new heart I will give you, and a new spirit I will put within you; and I will remove from your body the heart of stone and give you a heart of flesh. I will put my spirit within you, and make you follow my statutes and be careful to observe my ordinances" (Ezek 36:25–27).

D. E. H. Whiteley has a fascinating discussion of this point in terms of St. Paul's struggle over the failure of Israel to accept their messiah:

> St. Paul believed that two things were necessary for salvation: neither was effective alone, but both were essential. In the technical language of logic each was a necessary but not sufficient condition. If a woman wishes to light a gas-jet she must both turn on the gas and also strike a match. The match and the turning on of the gas are each necessary but not sufficient condition. For salvation it was

---

movement as reflected in the Wesleyan Theological Society. See Dunning, "A Wesleyan Perspective on Spirit Baptism."

necessary in St. Paul's thought both to have a covenant with God and to observe its terms. The covenant was a necessary condition, but not sufficient without obedience . . . The Jews had been given a covenant, but not the power to observe its terms, although such a power is promised in Ezek xxxvi. 27.

We may now see most fully the significance of the whole Christ event constituting the atonement in relation to this enabling provision of the new covenant. There is a vital connection between the totality of this event and the new reality of the Holy Spirit that became available as a result of it. The same power that sustained Jesus throughout his ministry enabling him to complete the task his Father had given him to do is now—through him—made available to those who identify with him in faith. This is the promise of the Father that Jesus instructed his followers to expect after they had tarried in Jerusalem.

The early Christian experience of the Holy Spirit, frequently described as being filled with the Spirit had certain inaugural characteristics but essentially it was a relationship shaped and energized by the experience of Jesus himself. J. H. E. Hull captures this perspective in his contrast between the pre-Christological and the post-Christological experience of being filled with the Holy Spirit:

> We may say for the moment that it was the same Spirit, the Holy Spirit Himself, who filled Elizabeth and Zechariah and the disciples also. But while Elizabeth and Zechariah were only able to feel that they were filled with the Spirit of One whom they had not seen, namely God, the disciples were aware that they were filled with the Spirit who had been in One they had seen, namely, in Christ Himself.[17]

A careful study of the early chapters of Acts will demonstrate the inseparable connection between the two benefits of the kingdom age included in the sixth point of Dodd's listing of the elements of the early church's preaching (see above). The focal point is 2:38, Peter's response to the Spirit-awakened question of his hearers: "Repent, and be baptized every one of you in the name of Jesus Christ so that your sins may be forgiven; and you will receive the gift of the Holy Spirit."

The appropriate response of those who were convicted through Peter's message involves three interrelated items. The first is repentance. The term here carries its literal meaning of a change of mind. The whole movement of the Gospels to the resurrection and ascension leads to this conclusion.

17. Hull, *The Holy Spirit in the Acts of the Apostles*, 68.

The great mystery that continually perplexed Jesus' disciples had finally been resolved in a complete reorientation of the so-called messianic hope. To acknowledge that a crucified carpenter could be God's messiah entailed a Copernican revolution in theology. This repentance was to be enacted by submitting to baptism in the name of Jesus so that through him the eschatological fulfillment could become an existential reality.

This baptism included both the forgiveness of sins *and* the gift of the Holy Spirit. Their correlation demonstrates unequivocally the fact that what was offered under the old covenant continues to be available, but now explicitly accompanied by what was absent under the old. As Bruner properly states it: "The forgiveness covers our major problem; the gift brings our major provision."[18] And that gift comes in and through Jesus Christ (incarnation) and his completed work (atonement).

---

18. Bruner, *Theology of the Holy Spirit*, 169.

Bibliography

Articles

Baab, Otto J. "The God of Redeeming Grace." *Interpretation* 10.2 (1956) 131–43.
Baloian, Bruce. "The Spirit of God in the Old Testament." In *The Spirit and the New Age*, edited by R. Larry Shelton and Alex R. G. Deasley, 3–32. Anderson, Indiana: Warner Press, Inc., 1972.
Bollier, John A. "The Righteousness of God." *Interpretation* 8 (1954) 404–13.
Connell, J. Clement. "The Propitiatory Element in the Atonement." *Vox Evangelica 4* (1965) 28–42.
Dabney. D. Lyle. "'Justified by the Spirit': Soteriological Reflections on the Resurrection." *International Journal of Systematic Theology*, 3.1 (March, 2001) 46–67.
Dunning, H. Ray. "Perspective for a Wesleyan Systematic Theology." In *Wesleyan Theology Today* edited by Theodore Runyon, 51–55. Nashville: Kingswood Press, 1985.
———. "A Wesleyan Perspective on Spirit Baptism." In *Perspectives on Spirit Baptism*, edited by Chad Owen Brand, 181–240. Nashville: Broadman & Holman Publishers, 2004.
Forde, Gerhard O."The Exodus from Virtue to Grace." *Interpretation* 34.1 (January, 1980) 32–44.
Gorringe, T. J. "'Not Assumed is Not Healed' The Homoousion and Liberation." *Scottish Journal of Theology* 38.4 (1985) 481–90.
Greathouse, W. M. "Sanctification and the Christus Victor Motif in Wesleyan Theology." *Wesleyan Theological Journal* 7.1 (Spring, 1972) 47–59.
Gunton, Colin. "Two Dogmas Revisited: Edward Irving's Christology." *Scottish Journal of Theology* 41.3 (1988) 359–76.
Hart, Trevor. "Irenaeus, Recapitulation and Physical Redemption." In *Christ in Our Place*, edited by T. Hart and D. Thimell, 152–81. Allison Park, PA: Pickwick Publications, 1989.
King, Robert H. "Introduction: The Task of Theology." In *Christian Theology* edited by Robert H. King and Peter Hodgson, 1–34. Philadelphia: Fortress Press, 1985.
Little, H. Ganse. "Christ For Us and In Us." *Interpretation* 10.2 (1956) 144–56.
Lyons, George. "The Spirit in the Gospels." In *The Spirit and the New Age*, edited by R. Larry Shelton and Alex R. G. Deasley, 33–88. Anderson, Indiana: Warner Press, Inc., 1972.
McGrath, Alister. "The Moral Theory of the Atonement: An Historical and Theological Critique." *Scottish Journal of Theology* 38.2 (1985) 205–20.
Macintosh, D. E. "Two Important Books of Theology." *Religion in Life* 7.3 (1938) 460–61.
Maddux, Randy. "John Wesley and Eastern Orthodoxy: Influences, Convergences and Differences. *The Asbury Theological Journal* 45.2 (1990) 29–53.
Manson, T. W. "*Hilasterion*." *Journal of Theological Studies*, 46 (1945) 1–10.

Milgrom, Jacob. "Sacrifices and Offerings, OT." In *IDB*, supplementary volume, edited by Keith Crim, 763–71. Nashville: Abingdon (1976).

Morris, Leon. "The Meaning of *Hilasterion* in Romans 3:24." *New Testament Studies 2* (1955) 33–43.

Mueller, John T. "Luther's Doctrine of the Atonement." *Christianity Today*. (April 1, 1957) 10–14.

Outler, Albert. "The Place of Wesley in the Christian Tradition." In *The Place of Wesley in the Christian Tradition*, edited by Kenneth E. Rowe, 11–38. Metuchen, N.J.: Scarecrow Press, 1976.

Pelican, Jaroslav. "Fundamentalism and/or Orthodoxy." In *The Fundamentalist Phenomenon* edited by Normal J. Cohen, 3–21. Grand Rapids: Wm. B. Eerdmans Publishing Company, 1990.

Pollard, Arthur. "Anselm's Doctrine of the Atonement: An Exegesis and Critique of Cur Deus Homo." *The Churchman*, 109/4 (1995) 304–16.

Root, Michael. "Necessity and Unfittingness in Anselm's *Cur Deus Homo*." *Scottish Journal of Theology*, 40.2 (1987) 211–30.

Rust, Eric. "The Atoning Act of God in Christ." *Review and Expositor* 59.1 (1962) 57–70.

Shelton, R. Larry. "A Covenant Concept of Atonement." *Wesleyan Theological Journal*, 19.1 (Spring 1984) 91–108.

Snaith, Norman. "Righteousness." In *A Theological Word Book of the Bible*, edited by Alan Richardson, 202–4. N.Y.: The Macmillan Co., 1950.

Taylor, R. O. P. "Was Abelard an Exemplarist?" *Theology*, 31 (1935) 207–13.

Taylor, Willard. "Wrath." In *Beacon Dictionary of Theology*, edited by Richard S. Taylor, et. al., 552–53. K. C.: Beacon Hill Press of Kansas City, 1983.

Thimell, Daniel P. "Christ in Our Place in the Theology of John McLeod Campbell," in *Christ in Our Place*, edited by T. Hart and D. Thimell, 182–206. Allison Park, PA: Pickwick Publications, 1989.

Torrance, James B. "Covenant or Contract? A Study of the Theological Background of Worship in Seventeenth Century Scotland" *Scottish Journal of Theology*, 23 (1970) 51–76.

———. "The Incarnation and Limited Atonement." *Evangelical Quarterly*, 55 (1983) 83–94.

Wright, N. T. "Justification." In *New Dictionary of Theology*, edited by David F. Wright, et. al., 359–61. http://www.ntwrightpage.com/Wright_NDCT-Justification.htm.

Books

Anderson, Bernhard. *Contours of Old Testament Theology*. Minneapolis: Fortress Press, 1999.

———. *Out of the Depths*. Philadelphia: Westminster Press, 1983.

Anderson, Ray S. *On Being Human*. Grand Rapids: Wm. B. Eerdmans Pub. Co., 1982.

Anselm. *Cur Deus Homo* in *St. Anselm, Basic Writings*. Translated by S. N. Deane. La Salle, IL: Open Court Publishing Co., n.d.

Athanasius. *De Incarnatione Verbe Dei*. Translated by T. Herbert Brindley. London: Religious Tract Society, n.d.

Aulén, Gustav. *Christus Victor*. N.Y.: The Macmillan Co., 1961.

Baillie, Donald. *God was in Christ*. London: Faber and Faber, Ltd., 1961.

Bangs, Carl. *Arminius*. Nashville: Abingdon Press, 1971.

Bibliography

Bright, John. *The Authority of the Old Testament*. Grand Rapids: Baker Book House, Twin Books, 1975.
———. *The Kingdom of God*. New York: Abingdon Press, 1953.
Brown, Joanne Carlson & Carole R. Bohn, editors. *Christianity, Patriarchy, and Abuse: A Feminist Critique*. New York: Pilgrim Press, 1989.
Calvin, John. *Institutes of the Christian Religion*. Translated by Henry Beveridge, 2 vols. London: James Clarke & Co. Ltd., 1949.
Cell, George Croft. *The Rediscovery of John Wesley*. N.Y.: Henry Holt and Co., 1935.
Chalke, S. and A. Mann. *The Lost Message of Jesus*. Grand Rapids: Zondervan Publishing Co., 2003.
Culpepper, Robert. *Interpreting the Atonement*. Grand Rapids: Wm. B. Eerdmans Pub. Co., 1966.
Dale, R. W. *The Atonement*. London: Congregational Union of England & Wales, 1905.
Davies, W. D. *Paul and Rabbinic Judaism*. Philadelphia: Fortress Press, 1980.
Denney, James. *The Death of Christ*. London: Hodder and Stoughton, 1902.
Deschner, John. *Wesley's Christology*. Grand Rapids: Francis Asbury Press, 1988.
Dillistone, F. W. *The Christian Understanding of the Atonement*. Philadelphia: Westminster Press, 1968.
———. *Jesus Christ and His Cross*. Philadelphia: Westminster Press, 1953.
Dodd, C. H. *The Apostolic Preaching of the Cross*. N.Y.: Harper & Bros. Publishers, 1962.
———. *The Epistle of Paul to the Romans*. London: Collier, 1959.
Driver, John. *Understanding the Atonement for the Mission of the Church*. Scottsdale, PA: Herald Press, 1986.
Dunning, H. Ray. *Grace, Faith and Holiness*. Kansas City: Beacon Hill Press of Kansas City, 1988.
———. *Reflecting the Divine Image*. Downers Grove, IL: Inter-Varsity Press, 1998.
Eichrodt, Walther. *Theology of the Old Testament*, 3 vols. Translated by J. A. Baker. Philadelphia: Westminster Press, 1961.
Fiddes, Paul. *Past Event and Present Salvation*. Louisville: Westminster/John Knox, 1989.
Foley, G. C. *Anselm's Theory of the Atonement*. London: Longmans, Green and Co., 1909.
Forsyth, P. T. *The Cruciality of the Cross*. Paternoster Press Biblical Classics, 1997.
———. *The Person and Place of Jesus Christ*. Grand Rapids: Eerdmans Publishing Co., n.d.
Franks, R. S. *The Work of Christ*. London: Thomas Nelson and Sons, Ltd, 1962.
Gese, Hartmut. *Essays in Biblical Theology*. Translated by Keith Crim. Minneapolis: Fortress Press, 1981.
Goldengay, J., ed. *Atonement Today*. London: SPCK, 1995.
Gonzalez, Justo. *Christian Thought Revisited*. Nashville: Abingdon Press, 1989.
Gould, J. Glenn. *The Precious Blood of Christ*. Kansas City: Beacon Hill Press of Kansas City, 1959.
Green, Joel B. & Mark D. Baker, *Recovering the Scandal of the Cross*. Downers Grove, IL: Intervarsity Press, 2000.
Grensted, L. W. *A Short History of the Doctrine of the Atonement*. Manchester: Manchester University Press, reprinted 1962.
Grider, J. Kenneth. *A Wesleyan-Holiness Theology*. Kansas City: Beacon Hill Press of Kansas City, 1994.
Gunton, Colin. *The Actuality of the Atonement*. Grand Rapids: Eerdmans Publishing Co., 1989.
———. *Christ and Creation*. Grand Rapids: Eerdmans Publishing Co., 1992.
Hendry, George S. *The Gospel of the Incarnation*. London: SCM Press, 1959.

Bibliography

———. *The Holy Spirit in Christian Theology*. Philadelphia: Westminster Press, 1965.
Heron, Alasdair I. C. *The Holy Spirit*. Philadelphia: Westminster Press, 1983.
Hill, David. *Greek Words and Hebrew Meanings*. Cambridge: Cambridge University Press, 1967.
Huegel, F. J. *Bone of His Bone*. Grand Rapids: Zondervan Publishing House, n.d.
Hull, J. H. E. *The Holy Spirit in the Acts of the Apostles*. Cleveland: World Publishing Co., 1968.
Johnson, Harry. *The Humanity of the Saviour*. London: The Epworth Press, 1962.
Kelly, J. N. D. *Early Christian Doctrines*. San Francisco: Harper and Row, Publishers, 1978.
Kerr, Hugh T., editor. *A Compend of Luther's Theology*. Philadelphia: The Westminster Press, 1966.
Ladd, George Eldon. *A Theology of the New Testament*, Revised Edition. Grand Rapids: Wm. B. Eerdmans Pub. Co., 1993.
Lindström, Harald. *Wesley and Sanctification*. Wilmore, KY: Frances Asbury Publishing Co., n.d.
McDonald, H. D. *The Atonement of the Death of Christ: In Faith, Revelation, and History*. Grand Rapids: Baker, 1985,
McGrath, Alister. *Christian Theology, An Introduction*. Oxford: Blackwell, 1994.
Macmurray, John. *Persons in Relation*. London: Faber & Faber, 1961
———. *The Self as Agent*. London: Faber & Faber, 1966
Maddux, Randy. *Responsible Grace*. Nashville: Kingswood Books, 1994.
Mann, Alan. *Atonement for a "Sinless Society:" Engaging with an Emerging Culture*. Milton Keynes: Paternoster, 2005.
Marsden, George M. *Fundamentalism and American Culture*. New York: Oxford University Press, 1980.
Martens, Elmer. *God's Design*. Grand Rapids: Baker, 1981.
Moberly, R. C. *Atonement and Personality*. London: John Murray, 1917.
Moody, Dale. *Word of Truth: A Summary of Christian Doctrine Based on Biblical Revelation*. Grand Rapids: Eerdmans Publishing Co., 1981.
Morgan, James. *The Importance of Tertullian in the Development of Christian Dogma*. London: K. Paul, Trench, Teubner, 1928.
Morris, Leon. *The Apostolic Preaching of the Cross*. Grand Rapids: Eerdmans Publishing Co., 1955.
Oden, Thomas. *Word of Life*. N.Y.; Harper & Row, Pub., 1989.
Outler, Albert. *Theology in the Wesleyan Spirit*. Nashville: Tidings, 1975.
Pannenberg, Wolfhart. *Jesus—God and Man*. Translated by Lewis L. Wilkins and Duane A. Priebe. Philadelphia: Westminster Press, 1966.
Parker, Rebecca Ann & Rita Nakashima Brock. *Proverbs of Ashes: Violence, Redemptive Suffering, and the Search for What Saves Us*. Boston: Beacon Press, 2001.
Richardson, Alan. *An Introduction to the Theology of the New Testament*. New York: Harper & Bros., Publishers, 1958.
Ridderbos, Herman. *Paul: An Outline of His Theology*. Translated by John Richard De Witt. Grand Rapids: Eerdmans Publishing Co., 1975.
Rowley, H. H. *The Meaning of Sacrifice in the Old Testament*. John Rylands Library Bulletin, vol. 33, No. 1. September, 1950.
Schleiermacher, F. D. E. *The Christian Faith*. Edinburgh: T. and T. Clark, 1960.
Seeberg, Reinhold. *Text-Book of the History of Doctrines*. Translated by Charles E. Hay. Grand Rapids: Baker Book House, 1964.

Bibliography

Siggins, Jim. *Martin Luther's Doctrine of Christ*. New Haven: Yale University Press, 1907.
Snaith, Norman. *Distinctive Ideas of the Old Testament*. London: The Epworth Press, 1955.
Sprague, C. Joseph. *Affirmations of a Dissenter*. Nashville: Abingdon Press, 2002.
Swartley, Willard. *Violence Renounced*. Telford, PA: Pandora Press, 2000.
Swete, H. B. *The Holy Spirit in the New Testament*. Grand Rapids: Baker Book House, 1964.
Stewart, James S. *A Man in Christ*. N.Y.: Harper & Row, Pub., n.d.
Tannehill, Robert C. *Dying and Rising With Christ*. Berlin: Verlag Alfred Töpelmann, 1967.
Taylor, Richard S. *God's Integrity and the Cross*. Nappanee, IN: Francis Asbury Press, 1999.
Taylor, Vincent. *The Atonement in New Testament Teaching*. London: Epworth Press, 1963.
———. *Jesus and His Sacrifice: A Study of the Passion-Sayings in the Gospels*. London: Macmillan & Co. 1937.
Temple, William. *Nature, Man and God*. London: The Macmillan Co., 1934.
Tillich, Paul. *Systematic Theology*, 3 vols. in 1. Chicago: University of Chicago Press, 1967.
Torrance, Thomas F., editor. *The Incarnation*. Edinburgh: The Handsel Press, 1981.
Travis, Stephen. *Christ and Judgment of God: Divine Retribution in the New Testament*. Basingstoke: Marshall Pickering, 1986.
Tuttle, George M. *So Rich a Soil*. Edinburgh: The Handsel Press, 1986.
Van Buren, Paul. *Christ in Our Place*. Grand Rapids: Eerdmans Publishing Co., n.d.
Wallace, Ronald. *The Atoning Death of Christ*. Westchester, ILL: Crossway Books, n. d.
Weaver, J. Denny. *The Non-Violent Atonement*. Grand Rapids: Eerdmans Publishing Co., 2001.
Wesley, John. *Letters of the Reverend John Wesley*. Edited by John Telford, 8 vols. London: Epworth Press, 1931.
———. *Explanatory Notes on the New Testament*. London: The Epworth Press, 1954.
———. *The Works of John Wesley*, 14 vols. Kansas City: Beacon Hill Press of Kansas City; reproduction of the 1872 edition, n.d.
Whiteley, D. E. H. *The Theology of Paul*. Oxford: Basil Blackwell, 1964.
Willard, Dallas. *The Divine Conspiracy*. San Francisco: Harper, 1998.
Wiley, H. Orton. *Christian Theology*, 3 vols. Kansas City: Beacon Hill Press of Kansas City, 1940–943.
Williams, Colin. *John Wesley's Theology Today*. N.Y.: Abingdon Press, 1960.
Young, Robert. *Analytical Concordance to the Bible*. New York: Funk & Wagnalls Company, n.d.
Ziesler, J. A. *The Meaning of Righteousness in Paul*. Cambridge: University Press, 1972.

Unpublished Material

Dunning, H. Ray, "The Concept of Original Sin in Justin Martyr and Irenaeus." M.A. thesis, Vanderbilt University, 1952.
Knight, John A. "The Theology of John Fletcher." PhD diss., Vanderbilt University, 1966.
Renshaw, Charles Allen. "The Atonement in the Theology of John and Charles Wesley." PhD diss., Boston University, 1965.

www.ingramcontent.com/pod-product-compliance
Lightning Source LLC
Chambersburg PA
CBHW072155160426
43197CB00012B/2399